Red Hat® Linux® 6

fast&easy™

Rave reviews for PRIMA TECH's *fast & easy* series

"Excellent book! Easy to read, easy to comprehend, easy to implement!"
Cheryl Johnson
Reno, NV

"Fantastic! Remarkably to the point, yet not once does it neglect vital information."
Joshua Loop
Cincinnati, OH

"Excellent book. Easy to understand!"
Cay Colberg
Albuquerque, NM

"The best book I've found!"
Bertha Podwys
Iverness, FL

"Great for fast reference!"
Janet White
Orlando, FL

"Well presented, concise, and extremely helpful!"
Julia Kogut
Arlington, VA

"So well illustrated that one couldn't possibly fail to profit from its content."
Charles Bendal
Surrey, England

"Very thorough and easy to use."
Cathy Mercer
Clifton, TX

"This book dispels the myth that computing is complicated."
Iain Clark
Durham, England

Send Us Your Comments

To comment on this book or any other PRIMA TECH title, visit our reader response page on the Web at **www.prima-tech.com/comments**.

How to Order

For information on quantity discounts, contact the publisher: Prima Publishing, P.O. Box 1260BK, Rocklin, CA 95677-1260; (916) 632-4400. On your letterhead, include information concerning the intended use of the books and the number of books you wish to purchase. For individual orders, visit PRIMA TECH's Web site at **www.prima-tech.com**.

Red Hat® Linux® 6

fast&easy™

Coletta Witherspoon

and

Craig Witherspoon

A DIVISION OF PRIMA PUBLISHING

A Division of Prima Publishing

Prima Publishing and colophon are registered trademarks of Prima Communications, Inc. PRIMA TECH and Fast & Easy are trademarks of Prima Communications, Inc., Rocklin, California 95677.

Publisher: Stacy L. Hiquet

Associate Publisher: Nancy Stevenson

Managing Editor: Dan J. Foster

Senior Acquisitions Editor: Deborah F. Abshier

Acquisitions Editor: Kim Spilker

Project Editor: Kevin W. Ferns

Editorial Assistant: Brian Thomasson

Copy Editor: Judy Ohm

Technical Editor: Van Hendrickson

Interior Design and Layout: Marian Hartsough Associates

Cover Design: Prima Design Team

Indexer: Katherine Stimson

ISBN: 0-7615-2158-5
Library of Congress Catalog Card Number: 99-64308
Printed in the United States of America

99 00 01 02 03 DD 10 9 8 7 6 5 4 3

To Craig's mom, Gwen

Acknowledgments

We'd like to thank everyone at PRIMA TECH for their continued support. It is always a pleasure to work with such a talented and dedicated group of people. We'd especially like to thank Nancy Stevenson for offering us this opportunity, Kim Spilker for getting us the tools we needed to get the job done, Kevin Ferns for keeping this book project on track, Judy Ohm for doing such a great edit job, Van Hendrickson for checking the technical accuracy of our manuscript, and Brian Thomasson for showing no fear the first time he installed Linux.

About the Author

COLETTA and **CRAIG WITHERSPOON** have been involved in the growth of the computer revolution from the beginning. They began writing procedure manuals for network administrators and managers, disaster and recovery plans for international corporations, and hardware and software training manuals for network users in the 1970s. Coletta and Craig have published over a dozen books, and Coletta is the author of several *Fast & Easy* series books from PRIMA TECH.

Contents at a Glance

Contents

PART III
MAKING LINUX WORK FOR YOU 179

Introduction

This *Fast & Easy* series guide from Prima Tech will help you to quickly gain an understanding of the Red Hat Linux 6.0 operating system and use it to your best advantage. You'll learn about GNOME, the graphical user interface that makes it easy for you to configure your computer and use the Linux features and programs. The GNOME built-in desktop tools and applications work together with standard conventions to allow applications to cooperate with each other. The powerful graphics-driven GNOME environment will make Red Hat Linux 6.0 seem very familiar to users of other operating systems.

This book will help you quickly navigate your way through the maze of tasks associated with learning a new operating system and show you how to make Red Hat Linux 6.0 a friendly and exciting new addition to your computing world. In an easy step-by-step fashion, this *Fast & Easy* guide will get you up and running with Red Hat Linux 6.0 in no time.

Who Should Read This Book?

As you thumb through this book, you'll find that it is filled with easy-to-follow directions and illustrations that show you what you'll see on your screen as you progress through the directions. This book is the perfect tool for those who are familiar with other computer operating systems and want to get up to speed with Red Hat Linux 6.0 and the GNOME graphical user interface. You may need to read all of the individual chapters in a particular section of the book to master its subject matter, or you may only need to read certain chapters to fill any gaps in your existing knowledge. This book is structured to support the method that suits you best.

Red Hat Linux 6 Fast & Easy also makes a great reference tool. As you work with Red Hat 6.0 and learn new things, you may sometimes need a quick reminder about how to perform a specific task or configure a new peripheral. You can easily and quickly refer to those things in this book.

Helpful Hints to Increase Your Skills

Included in this book are additional elements that will provide you with more information on how to work with Red Hat Linux 6.0 and the GNOME graphical user interface without encumbering your progress:

- Tips offer shortcuts for various Linux and GNOME features, to make your job a little easier.

- Notes offer additional information about a feature or advice on how to use the feature.

The appendix shows you how to install Red Hat Linux 6.0.

Have fun with this *Fast & Easy* guide. It's the quickest and simplest way to get started with the Linux operating system.

PART I

Getting Started with Linux and GNOME

1

Discovering Linux

Congratulations! You've decided to take the plunge and give Linux a try. One of the newest additions to the Red Hat Linux distribution is the GNOME user interface. GNOME makes it easier for you to get familiar with this new operating system. GNOME uses graphical elements such as icons and menus to open applications, perform tasks, and navigate around the screen. Before you begin, take the time to create a user account. Then, sit back and explore GNOME. In this chapter, you'll learn how to:

- Start the Linux operating system and GNOME
- Create a user account for your daily Linux activities
- Use the different GNOME screen elements
- Find additional help using Linux and GNOME
- Exit GNOME and Linux

Starting Linux for the First Time

When you installed Linux on your computer (if you haven't yet installed Linux, see the appendix in the back of this book), the installation set up your computer so that anyone with the installation password can log in as the superuser (using root as the user ID) and have access to the entire operating system. This can be dangerous. The person in charge of the computer should set up a user account for each person who will be using the system. Then, each user can use Linux according to their personal preferences.

Creating a New User

When you installed Linux, you were given the option to start a program called "X" when your computer reboots. If you selected this option, you'll automatically see the GNOME interface on your screen. If you decided not to start X automatically, or if there was a problem during the X configurator process, you'll see the *localhost login* prompt. This is your cue that Linux is ready for you to begin. This section will show you how to get to a GNOME terminal window so that you can create a user account for yourself. This is done from the superuser account (or root) of your Linux operating system. You'll only want to use this superuser account to perform system administration and maintenance. Your user account is where you should be working with GNOME and other applications.

CAUTION

Be careful when you are logged into the system as root. The root user account has total access to the entire Linux operating system.

NOTE
If you see GNOME on your screen, skip steps 1 through 3.

```
Red Hat Linux release 6.0 (Hedwig)
Kernel 2.2.5-15 on an i586
localhost login: root
Password: _
```

1. Type root at the localhost login: prompt and **press** the **Enter key**. The Password: prompt will appear.

2. Type the **password** that you chose during the installation process and **press** the **Enter key**. A message will appear showing when you last logged into your Linux system and the [root@localhost /root]# prompt will display.

```
Red Hat Linux release 6.0 (Hedwig)
Kernel 2.2.5-15 on an i586
localhost login: root
Password:
Last login: Thu Apr 29 22:25:46 on
tty2
[root@localhost /root]# startx
```

3. Type the command **startx**. Then **press** the **Enter key**. The Enlightenment Window Manager will load and GNOME will appear on your screen.

4. **Click** on the **GNOME Terminal emulation program button** on the GNOME Panel. The GNOME Terminal window will open.

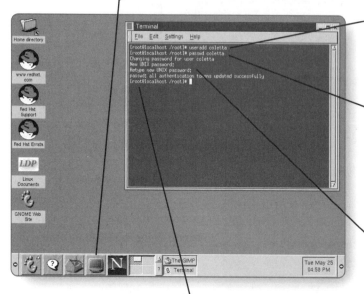

5. **Type** the command **useradd**, a **space**, and a **user name** for yourself. Then press the Enter key.

6. **Type** the command **passwd**, a **space**, and the **user name** you created in step 3 and then **press** the **Enter key**. The New UNIX password prompt will appear on the next line.

7. **Type** a **password** and **press** the **Enter key**. The Retype new UNIX password prompt will appear.

8. **Retype** the **password** from step 5 and **press** the **Enter** key. You'll be returned to the root prompt. You'll see a note that the password authentication was successful.

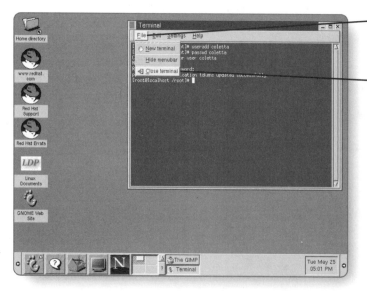

9. **Click** on **File**. The File menu will appear.

10. **Click** on **Close terminal**. The GNOME Terminal window will close.

11. **Click** on the **Main Menu button**. The Main Menu will appear.

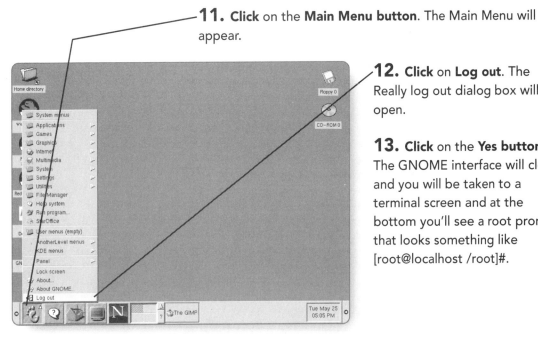

12. **Click** on **Log out**. The Really log out dialog box will open.

13. **Click** on the **Yes button**. The GNOME interface will close and you will be taken to a terminal screen and at the bottom you'll see a root prompt that looks something like [root@localhost /root]#.

```
waiting for X server to shut down

[root@localhost /root]# logout
```

14. **Type logout** and **press** the **Enter key**. You'll return to the localhost login prompt.

```
Red Hat Linux release 6.0 (Hedwig)

Kernel 2.2.5-15 on an i586

localhost login: coletta

Password: _
```

15. **Type** the new **user name** and **password** that you just created. You'll see a prompt that looks like [username@localhost username]$. Now you're ready to start GNOME.

Getting to GNOME

Now that you're logged into your user account, it's time to open the GNOME desktop.

```
Red Hat Linux release 6.0 (Hedwig)

Kernel 2.2.5-15 on an i586

localhost login: coletta

Password:

[tempuser@localhost tempuser]$ startx
```

1. At the user prompt, **type startx** and **press** the **Enter key**. You'll see a status box showing the Enlightenment window manager loading. Then, GNOME will appear.

Exploring GNOME

When GNOME appears on your screen, you'll see the familiar icons and windows from the Windows and Macintosh operating systems; but some things may look different.

Understanding Desktop Elements

- The desktop is the background for all of the elements you see on your screen. You'll learn how to change the desktop background in Chapter 4, "Customizing the Screen Display."

- Desktop icons open applications, files, or directories quickly. You can place icons on your desktop for those programs and files you use frequently. Learn more about this in Chapter 4, "Customizing the Screen Display."

- Windows are framed areas that contain menus, buttons, and scroll bars. Applications and files appear inside windows. You'll find out how to resize a window in Chapter 2, "Working with Program Windows." Find out how to work with several windows at one time in Chapter 3, "Moving around Your Desktop."

The GNOME Panel resides at the bottom of your screen. The GNOME Panel contains the Main Menu button, a number of panel applets, and the GNOME Pager.

- The Main Menu button opens a menu of all the applications, utilities, and actions you can perform with GNOME. To display the menu, click on the Main Menu button (it's the foot at the far left). To close the menu, click on the Main Menu button a second time or click on an empty area of the desktop.

- Panel applets are small programs that can be started easily by clicking on the applet icon. You can add and delete applets from the panel. Learn how to do this in Chapter 4, "Customizing the Screen Display."

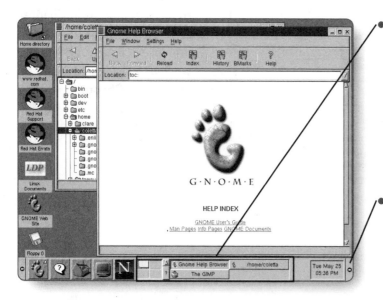

- The GNOME Pager shows you which applications and files are open on your computer and where they are located on the virtual desktops. You'll learn more about the GNOME Pager and virtual desktops in Chapter 3, "Moving around Your Desktop."

- At each end of the GNOME Panel, there's an arrow inside a circle. These arrows hide and display the GNOME Panel.

Starting Programs from the Main Menu Button

Now it's time to take a look at some of your software applications and get a quick overview of how to use the common window interface elements. The next few sections will show you how to use the basic elements of a Linux application by using the GNOME Calendar.

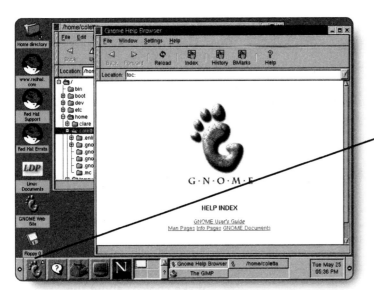

1. Click on the **Main Menu Button**. A menu will appear.

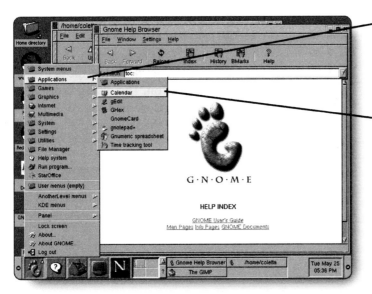

2. Move the **mouse pointer** over a menu item that has an arrow to the right of it. A second menu will appear.

3. Click on the **application** with which you want to work. The application window will appear on your screen.

Using Buttons, Menus, and Dialog Boxes

You've successfully opened a Linux application and now you're ready to see how it works. Program windows contain elements such as menus, command buttons, resize buttons, and a host of other elements. Take some time to explore the different menus to see what is available. This section will show you how to use buttons and menus to execute commands.

1. Place the **mouse pointer** over a button on the toolbar. The button will be highlighted and a tip will appear telling you what function the button performs.

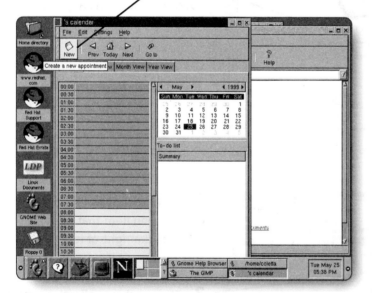

2. Click on a **button**. The command associated with the button will be executed. The command may be executed automatically or a dialog box will appear allowing you to make choices about the command you wish to execute.

NOTE

If you've opened a dialog box, click on the Close button. The dialog box will close and any choices you made in the dialog box will be ignored.

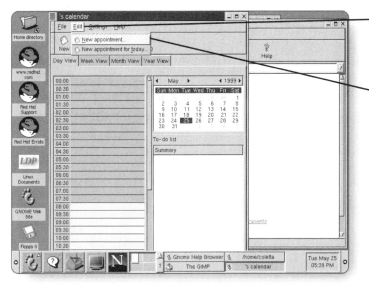

3. Click on a **menu item** to open a menu. A list of menu commands will appear.

4. Click on a **command**. A dialog box will open. Dialog boxes let you perform a variety of functions.

Dialog boxes contain buttons that display secondary dialog boxes, buttons that let you select options, lists that let you select a number of predefined options, and tabs that group several dialog boxes into one.

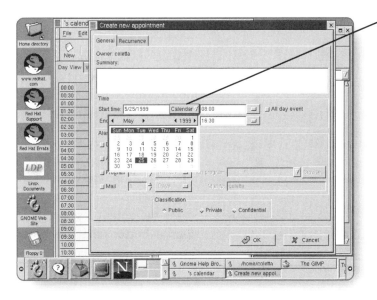

● Open applets from which you can perform a task or make a selection by clicking on the down arrow within the dialog box and clicking on applet elements to make your choice. The choice you make will appear in the text box next to the down arrow.

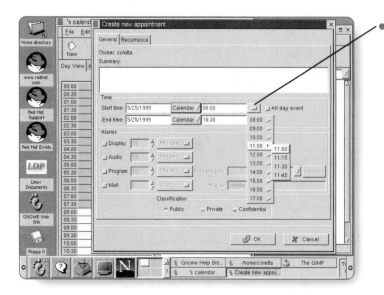

Open drop-down lists by clicking on the list button to display a list of options, and then click on the option you want. The choice you make will appear in the text box.

Turn features on and off by clicking on the selection box next to the feature name. The selection box will become recessed when the feature is turned on. The selection box is raised when the feature is turned off.

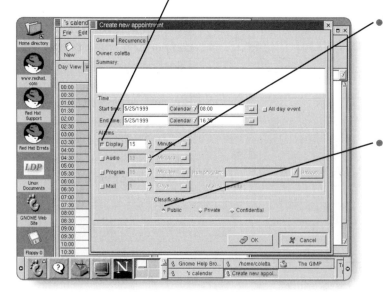

Adjust numbers by clicking on the up and down arrows. The up arrow will increase the number in the text box. The down arrow will decrease the number in the text box.

Select one of a group of options by clicking on the option button. The option button will become recessed when the option is selected. Option buttons that are raised are not selected.

● Find more options by clicking on a tab.

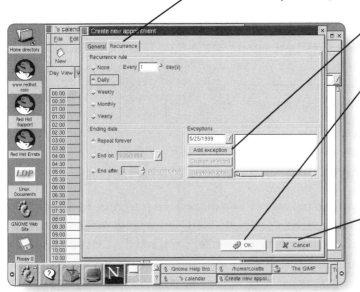

● Access a secondary dialog box by clicking on a button.

5. Click on **OK**. The dialog box will close and the options will be applied and you will be returned to the program window.

TIP

Click on Cancel if you don't wish to apply any of the changes you made to the dialog box or you decide that you no longer want to execute the command.

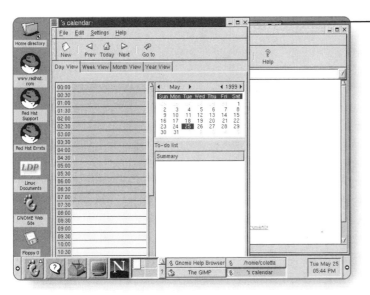

6. Click on the **Kill button** at the top right of the program window when you are finished working with the application. The application will close and you will be returned to the GNOME interface.

NOTE

If a window refuses to close, right-click on the Kill button. The application will be dumped and you can continue working. You can even open the same application and begin working with it again.

Getting Help

After reading this book, you'll feel comfortable using Linux with the GNOME interface. But this is just the beginning of your journey. As you get more involved in your new Linux operating system, you'll find new uses for some of the features you've learned about so far and discover new features that you'll want to explore.

Using the Mouse to Get Help

When you're looking for a quick answer to what function a button performs or how to work with a window, just place the mouse pointer over the element and see if a tool tip appears.

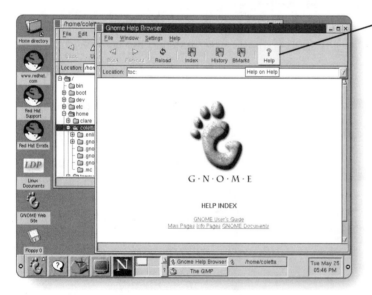

1. **Hold** the **mouse pointer** over a screen or window element. A tool tip will appear that gives more information about the element's function.

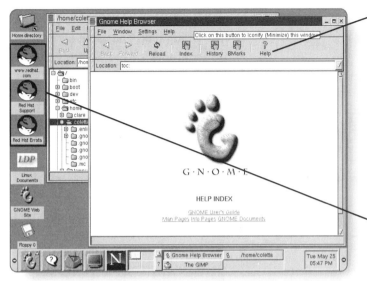

2. **Hold** the **mouse pointer** over a window element. A tool tip will appear that makes suggestions as to functions that can be applied to the window element and gives further instructions about how to perform a task.

> **NOTE**
>
> The icons at the left side of the desktop are links to the Red Hat Web site where you can find additional help.

Getting Help

The GNOME Help Browser is your one-stop place for all the Linux and GNOME help files. This help system does not contain a search feature. You'll need to read through the list of contents and click on the help topic that you want to read. This section will show you how to access and work with the GNOME User's Guide.

Browsing the Help Files

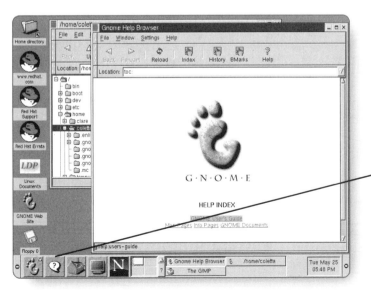

1. **Click** on the **Help button** if the GNOME Help Browser is not displayed on your screen. The GNOME Help Browser will appear displaying the Index page.

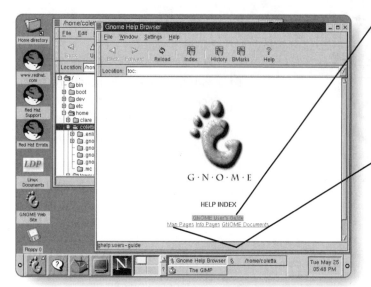

2. Click on the **GNOME User's Guide link**. The table of contents for the GNOME User's Guide will appear.

NOTE

After you become more familiar with Linux and want to know more about using Linux commands, you may want to check out the Man Pages. The Man Pages are notes written by Linux programmers that tell you how to use all the Linux commands. The Man Pages are the complete documentation package for all Linux distributions.

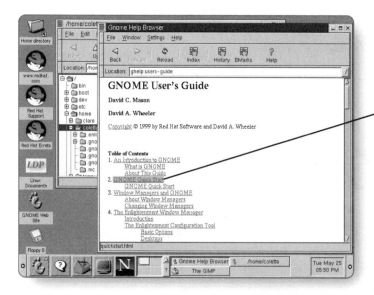

3. Read through the list of **topics** until you find the one that matches the information you need.

4. Click on the **link** for the help topic you want to read. If you want to read the user's guide from start to finish, click on An Introduction to GNOME link. The associated help file will appear in the browser.

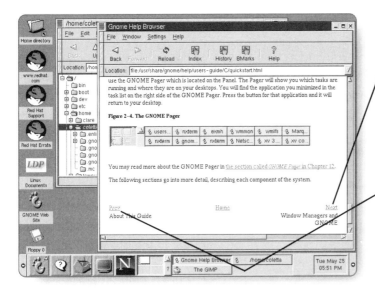

5. **Read** the **information** on the page.

6. **Click** on the **Next link** to read the next page from the list of contents. The next page in the user's guide will appear in the browser.

7. **Click** on the **Prev button** to go back to the previous page that you viewed. The last page that you viewed will appear in the browser.

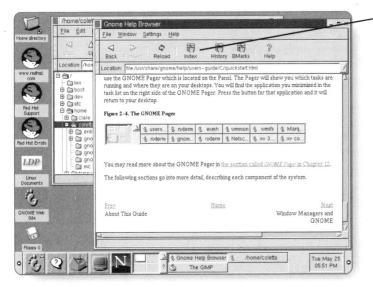

8. **Click** on the **Index button** to return to the main page of the user's guide. The title page of the GNOME User's Guide will appear in the browser.

Setting Bookmarks

When you find a page that contains useful information that you think you'll need again, you can set a bookmark to make it easy to find the information again. Or, if you're reading the user's guide from cover to cover and want to remember where you left off, mark the spot with a bookmark.

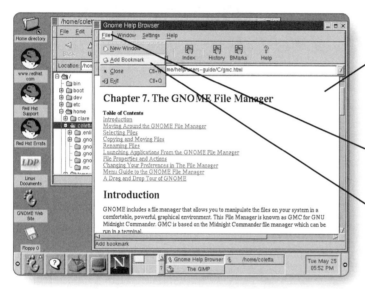

1. Open the **page** to which you want to set a bookmark in the browser window. The page will appear in the browser.

2. Click on **File**. The File menu will appear.

3. Click on **Add Bookmark**. A bookmark will be created for you.

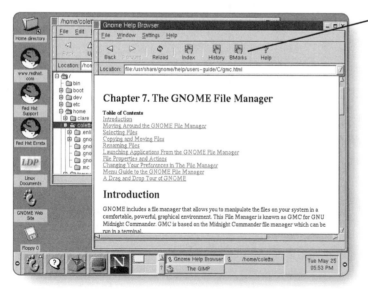

4. Click on the **BMarks button** if you want to display a help topic that you previously bookmarked. The GNOME Help Bookmarks dialog box will open.

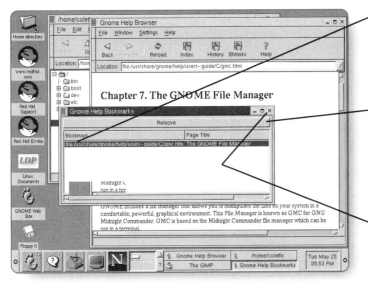

5. **Click** on the **help topic** that you want to read. The help topic will appear in the browser window.

6. To delete a bookmark, **select** the **bookmark** you want to remove and **click** on the **Remove button**. The bookmark will be removed from the list.

7. To close the bookmark window, **click** on the **Kill button**. The dialog box will close.

Finding Previously Viewed Help Files

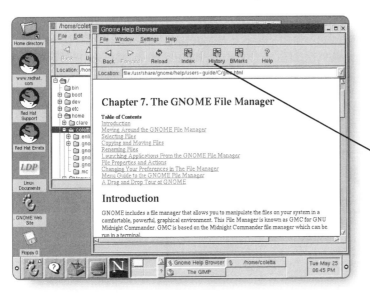

There may be times when you know you've read a help file but just can't remember where it was located. You can open a history list and see what help topics you viewed and when.

1. Click on the **History button**. The GNOME Help History dialog box will open.

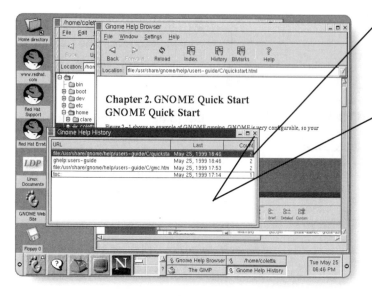

2. **Browse** through the **list** and **click** on the **help file** that you want to view. The help file will appear in the browser window.

3. **Click** on the **Kill button** when you are finished with the history list. The GNOME Help History dialog box will close.

Finding Help Files in Applications

You can also find help that is specific to the application or window in which you are working. If the application does not have a Help button, you can find help from the Help menu.

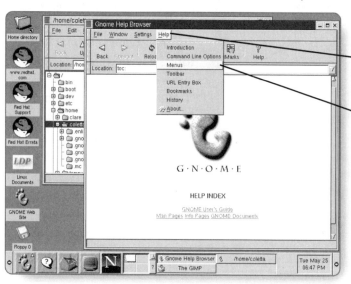

1. **Click** on **Help**. The Help menu will appear.

2. **Click** on the **topic** that you want to read about. A help file will appear in a browser window.

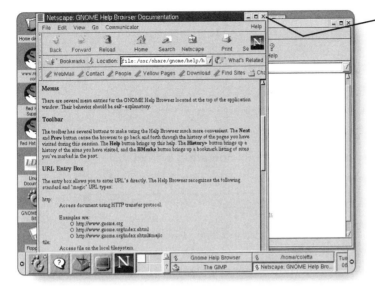

3. **Click** on the **Kill button** when you are finished reading the help file. The browser window will close.

Exiting Linux

When you are finished working with Linux, you'll want to log out of your user account so that others using the same computer will not have access to your user files and directories. You can also make sure that any settings you may have changed will be just the way you left them the next time you log into your user account.

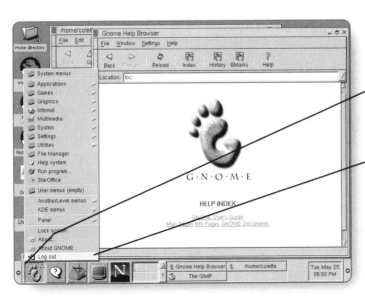

1. **Click** on the **Main Menu button**. The Main menu will appear.

2. **Click** on **Log out**. The Really log out? Dialog box will open.

3. **Click** on the **Logout option button**. The option will be selected.

NOTE

If you want to turn off your computer, click on the Halt button.

---

4. Click on **Yes**. GNOME will close and you will return to the user prompt in the Linux operating system.

TIP

If you want your screen to appear the same way it looked when you logged out, click on the Save current setup selection box.

```
waiting for X server to shut down

[tempuser@localhost tempuser]$ logout
```

5. Type logout and **press** the **Enter key**. The login screen will appear and the next user can log in without being able to access your user account.

2

Working with Program Windows

The screen element that you'll use often in the Linux operating system is the program window. A window is a boxed area on your screen where you do all your work. From a window, you can work with an application, view your computer's filing system, and perform computer maintenance tasks. You have the option of changing the size and appearance of each window with which you will be working. In addition, there are ways to customize the appearance of a window and how it displays on your screen. In this chapter, you'll learn how to:

- Open a window and change the way it opens on the screen
- Change the size of a window
- Move the window to a different place on the screen
- Close a window

Opening Program Windows

When you start an application, a window appears that contains the application and a number of elements that control the window's size. Take some time to learn how to manipulate a single screen. It will make it easier for you to work with the application and data inside the window. These skills will also help when you begin working with multiple windows.

Displaying a Program Window

It only takes a few mouse clicks to open a window. In this section, you'll learn to work with windows by opening the Gnumeric spreadsheet.

1. Click on the **Main Menu button**. The Main Menu will appear.

2. Move the **mouse pointer** to Applications. A second menu will appear.

3. Click on **Gnumeric spreadsheet**. The Gnumeric spreadsheet application will open displaying a blank workspace.

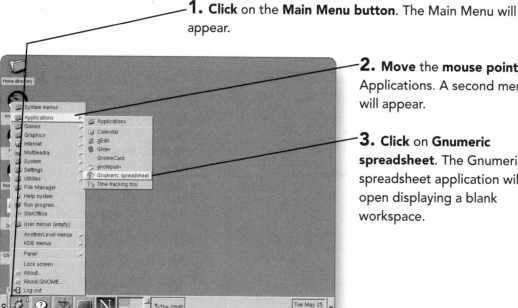

Most windows share a number of common elements that make it easy for you to move and resize a window.

- The Window Border menu contains all the commands that control the actions you can perform to an individual window.

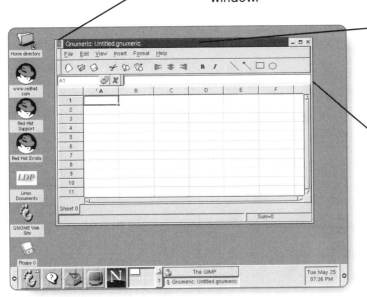

- The Drag bar tells you in which application you are working and also provides the easiest way to move a window around on your screen.

- The window border is a rim around the outside edge that you can use to resize the window.

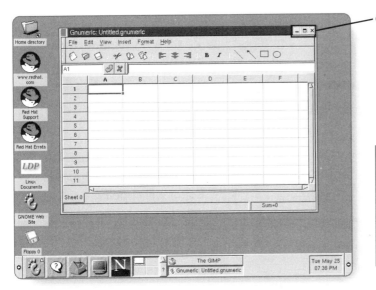

- The Minimize, Maximize, and Kill buttons will turn a window into an icon on the GNOME Pager, change the size of the window, and close the window.

NOTE

You can open an application from a desktop icon by double-clicking on the icon.

Making Windows Slide When Opened

By default, windows just pop open on the screen when a program or file is executed. If you would like to see the window grow while it opens, try out one of the different sliding methods. If you have an older computer with a slow processor, this feature may cause your system to react even slower.

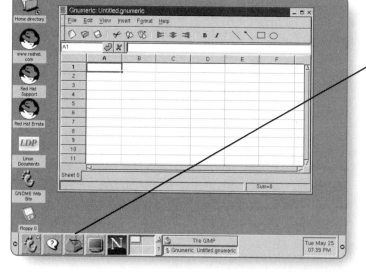

1. Click on the **GNOME Configuration Tool icon** on the GNOME Panel. The Control Center will appear.

NOTE

If you don't see this icon on the GNOME Panel, click on the Main Menu button, move the mouse pointer to Settings, then click on GNOME Control Center.

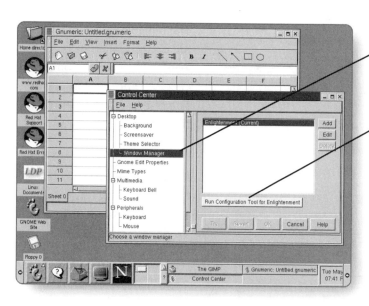

2. Click on **Window Manager**. The Window Manager pane will appear.

3. Click on the **Run Configuration Tool for Enlightenment button**. The Enlightenment Configuration Editor will appear.

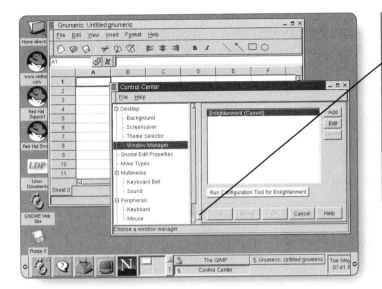

TIP

To change the size of the two panes in the Control Center, click and hold on the resize handle at the bottom of the bar between the two panes and drag in the direction that you want to resize the panes.

4. Click on **Special FX**. The Window Sliding Methods pane will appear.

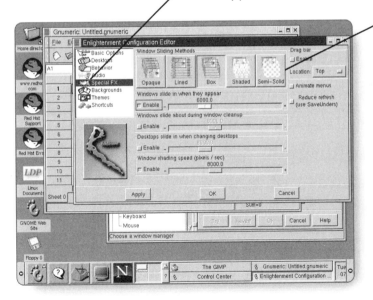

5. Click on a **Window Sliding Methods icon** that matches the way you would like to see windows open on your screen. The icon will be recessed.

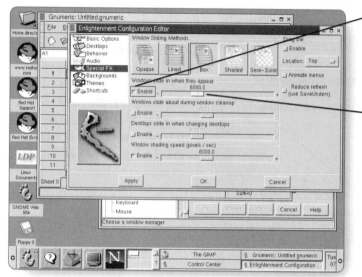

6. **Click** on an **Enable check button** in the Windows slide in when they appear area. The button will be recessed.

7. **Click** and **drag** the **slider** to change the amount of time it takes for the window to completely open. Dragging the slider to the right increases the amount of time it takes for the window to completely open. Dragging the slider to the left decreases the amount of time.

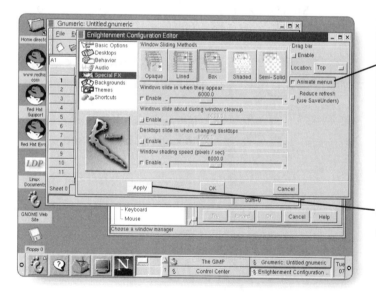

NOTE

If you want to change the way menus appear on your screen when they are opened, click on the Animate menus check button.

8. **Click** on **Apply**. Your changes will be applied.

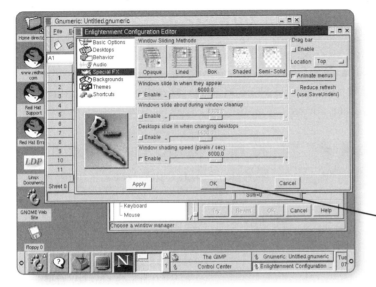

TIP

If you want to see your changes in action before you close the Enlightenment Configuration Editor, open a second application. If you don't like the effect, make some changes.

9. Click on **OK** when you are satisfied with the results. The Enlightenment Configuration Editor will close and the Control Center will appear.

10. Click on the **Kill button**. The Control Center will close.

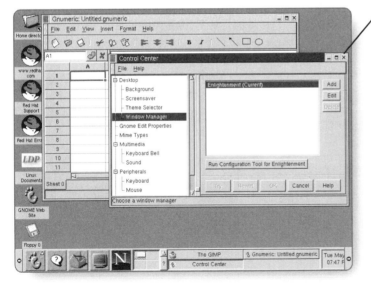

Resizing a Window

When a program window appears on your screen, it may not be in a size that is adequate for you to do your work. When this is the case, you'll need to resize the window. You have several options.

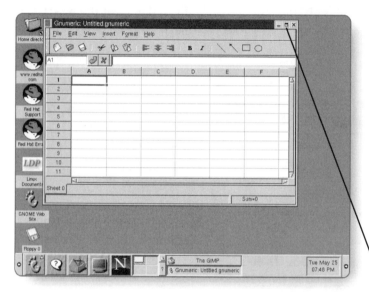

Using the Maximize Button

The easiest place to change the size of a window is with the Maximize button. The Maximize button is used to change the window from its smaller size so that it fills the screen. When you click on the Maximize button a second time, the window reverts to its original size.

1. **Click** on the **Maximize button** on a window that is smaller than the screen area. The window will fill the entire screen.

2. **Click** on the **Maximize button** on a window that fills the entire screen. The window will revert to its smaller, default size.

Using the Mouse

If you want more control over the size of a window, use the mouse. By dragging the window borders, you can create a window that is any size you need.

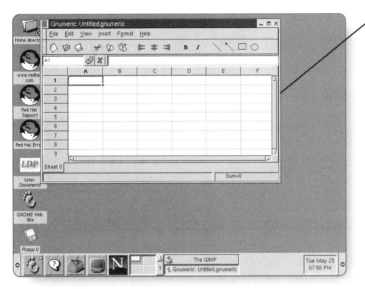

1. Click and **drag** either the **left** or **right window border**. Move the mouse pointer toward the window to make the window narrower. Move the mouse pointer away from the window to make the window wider. An outline of the window will appear.

2. Release the **mouse button** when the window is the desired size. The window will be resized.

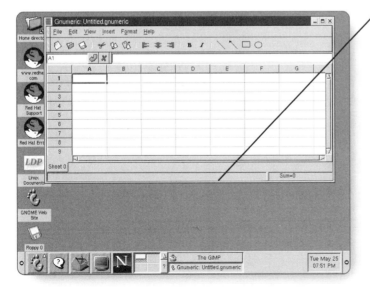

3. Click and **drag** the **bottom border**. Move the mouse pointer toward the window to make the window shorter. Move the mouse pointer away from the window to make the window longer. An outline of the window will appear.

4. Release the **mouse button** when the window is the desired size. The window will be resized.

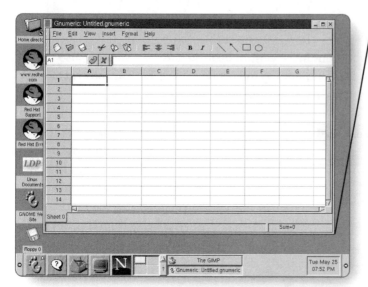

5. **Click** and **drag** the **bottom right** or **bottom left corner** of the window. Move the mouse pointer away from the window to make it wider and longer at the same time. Move the mouse pointer toward the window to make it shorter and narrower at the same time. An outline of the window will appear.

6. **Release** the **mouse button** when the window is the desired size. The window will be resized.

Changing the Windows Resize Display

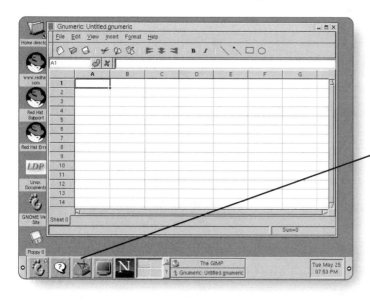

When you resize a window, you'll see an outline of the window while you are dragging a window border. You can change the outline from the Control Center.

1. **Click** on the **GNOME Configuration Tool icon** on the GNOME Panel. The Control Center will appear.

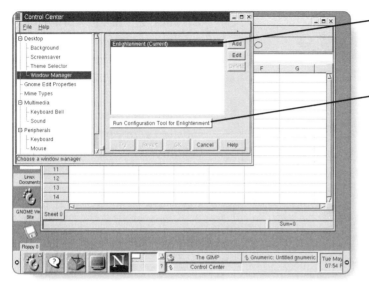

2. Click on **Window Manager**. The Window Manager pane will appear.

3. Click on the **Run Configuration Tool for Enlightenment button**. The Enlightenment Configuration Editor will appear.

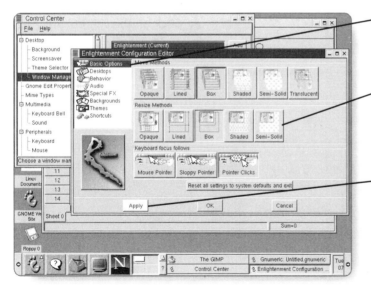

4. Click on **Basic Options**. The Basic Options pane will appear at the right side of the window.

5. Click on a **Resize Methods icon** that matches the resized outline you would like. The icon will be recessed.

6. Click on **Apply**. Your changes will be made.

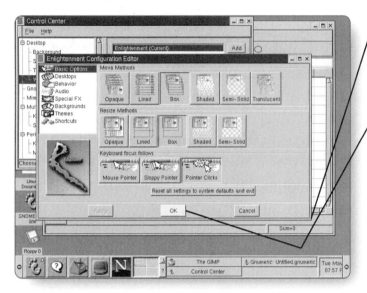

7. **Click** and **drag** a **corner** of the Enlightenment Configuration Editor window to see your changes in action.

8. **Click** on **OK** when you are satisfied with your changes. The Enlightenment Configuration Editor will close and the Control Center will appear.

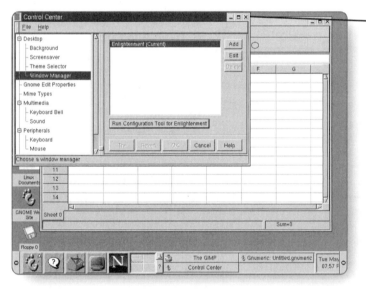

9. **Click** on the **Kill button**. The Control Center will close.

Turning Windows into Bars and Icons

You can hide a window on the screen without closing the program or window.

1. Click on the **Minimize button** at the right of the drag bar. The window will become an icon on the GNOME Pager.

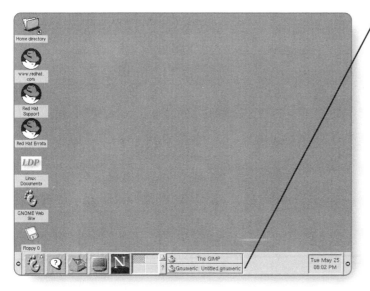

2. Click on the **icon** for the hidden window. The program window will open.

3. Double-click on the **Drag bar** located at the top of the program window. The program window will disappear (or shade) so that only the Drag bar is displayed.

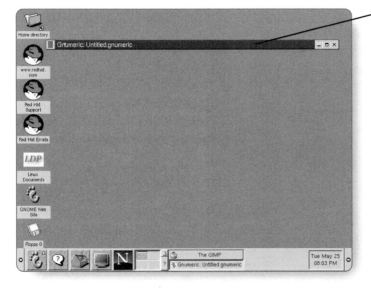

4. Double-click on the **Drag bar**. The window will unshade.

> ### NOTE
> You can click and drag the shaded Drag bar to any location on your screen.

5. **Click** on the **Windows Options menu** located on the left of the Drag bar. A menu of window functions will appear.

6. **Click** on **Iconify**. The program window will become an icon on the GNOME Pager.

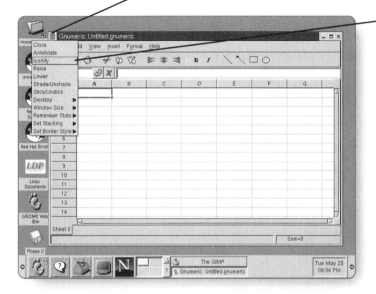

7. **Click** on the **program icon**. The program window will appear on your screen.

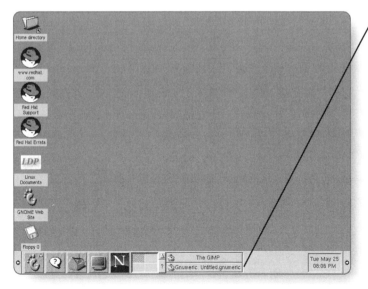

Moving a Window around the Screen

You may want to move a window around on your screen to make room for another program window. Or you may want to move it out of the way so that you can see something (like a program or shortcut icon) on your desktop.

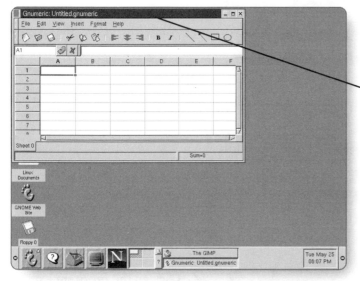

1. Click and **hold** the **Drag bar**. The window will be selected.

2. Drag the **window** to the desired position. You'll see the outline of the window as it moves.

3. Release the **mouse button** when the window is in the desired position. The window will be moved.

TIP

You can change the outline that appears when you drag program windows around the screen. Open the Enlightenment Configuration Editor. You'll find the resize methods in the Basic Options category.

Closing a Program Window

When you are finished looking at a program window, you can close it. If you've been working in the program (which you'll learn about in Chapter 10, "Working with Files"), you'll first need to save your work.

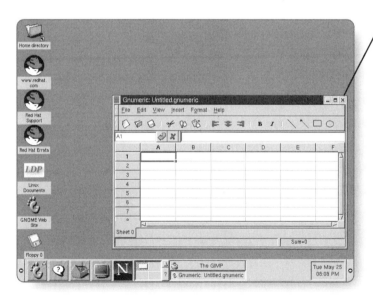

1. **Click** on the **Kill button** located at the far right of the Drag bar. The program window will close.

NOTE

If the window refuses to close, right-click on the Kill button.

3

Moving around Your Desktop

In the last chapter, you learned how to open a window and move it around on your desktop and you experimented with how to change the appearance and behavior of windows. One Linux strong suit is its multitasking capability. It is easy to work with multiple applications, multiple windows, and even multiple screens. You'll begin by opening and arranging multiple windows on a desktop area and then progress to using multiple desktop areas—which is like having more than one monitor on your desk. In this chapter, you'll learn how to:

- Arrange multiple screens on your desktop
- Move around between desktop areas with the GNOME Pager
- Change the number of desktop areas available on your desktop

Working with Multiple Windows

It's a simple task to open many applications, but keep in mind your computer's capabilities. It may not be as strong and powerful as your Linux. The multiple windows will pile on top of each other until it becomes hard to find a particular application window.

Finding a Few Applications to Open

One of the exciting features of your Linux system is the ability to multitask. Not only can you work with multiple applications at one time, but you can also group them on different desktop areas. Open a few windows on your desktop and experiment with the examples in this chapter.

1. **Click** on the **Main Menu Button**. The Main Menu will appear.

2. **Move** the **mouse pointer** to Applications. The Applications menu will appear.

3. **Click** on an **application**. The default program window for the application will open on your desktop area.

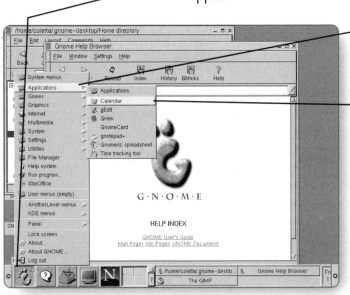

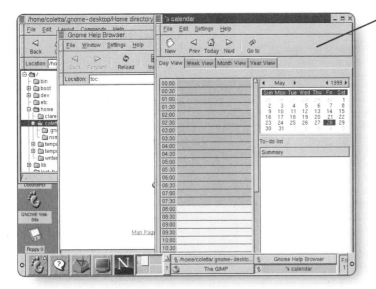

4. Repeat steps 1 through **3** until you have a half dozen open windows on your desktop area. The desktop will probably look cluttered and disorganized.

In this example, it may be hard to see, but there are seven open windows.

- By default, when you start GNOME, the file manager and the GNOME Help Browser windows will open.

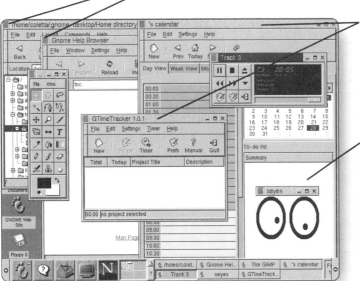

- The Calendar and the Time Tracking Tool can be found in the Applications menu. These are a couple of the productivity tools that you may find useful.

- There are a bunch of fun games to help you waste a little time (and practice your mouse skills, of course) in the Games menu.

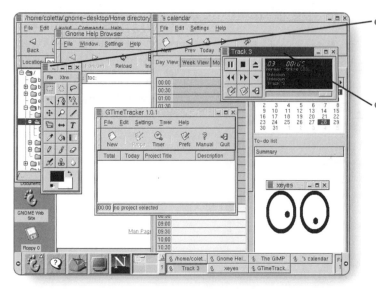

- If you feel artistic or want to enhance scanned images, look in the Graphics menu for The GIMP.

- When only tunes will get you through times of hard work, plug in the CD player and listen to the sound. You'll find the CD player in the Multimedia menu.

Cleaning Up Your Desktop

GNOME can organize the open windows. It will try to place open windows so that a portion of each window is visible on your screen.

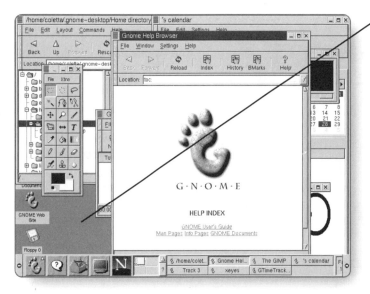

1. Find an **empty area** of the desktop and **click** the **left** and **right mouse buttons** simultaneously. A menu will appear.

NOTE

You may have to move one of the windows out of the way in order to find an empty space on the desktop background.

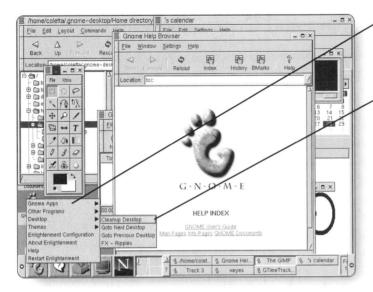

2. Move the **mouse pointer** to Desktop. The Desktop menu will appear.

3. Click on **Cleanup Desktop**. Your cluttered desktop will be organized.

You'll be able to see the drag bar on most of the open windows.

Shading and Organizing Windows

The automatic window arrangement may be less user-friendly than you'd like. You still have too many application windows to manage them efficiently or quickly find the one you want. Furthermore, your desk is still cluttered. Here's another trick for working with multiple applications and files at one time.

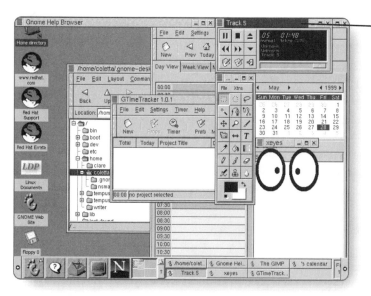

1. Double-click on the **drag bar** of one of the application windows. The window will become shaded by rolling up inside the drag bar.

2. Double-click on the **drag bars** of the other open windows on your desktop until all of the windows are shaded. Only the titles of the applications running in the window will show on the drag bar of each window.

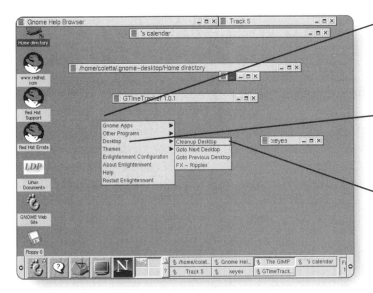

3. Click on the **right** and **left mouse buttons** simultaneously on an empty area of the desktop. A menu will appear.

4. Move the **mouse pointer** to Desktop. The Desktop menu will appear.

5. Click on **Cleanup desktop**. The shaded application windows will be organized into a list.

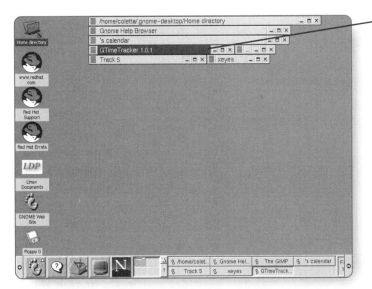

6. Double-click on the **drag bar** of the application with which you want to work. The application window will open.

NOTE

This can be a useful way to store windows temporarily when you need space on the desktop to work, but the real solution is to get more desktop areas.

Working with Multiple Desktop Areas

Linux is capable of using your video hardware to its maximum capabilities, as it can support a virtual screen size much larger than your actual monitor screen's dimensions. This large virtual screen can be divided into separate desktop areas. The GNOME Pager on the GNOME Panel can navigate from desktop area to desktop area and keep track of your applications.

Understanding the GNOME Pager

The GNOME Pager is an applet that runs inside the GNOME Panel. The GNOME Pager shows all the desktop areas and what applications are on them.

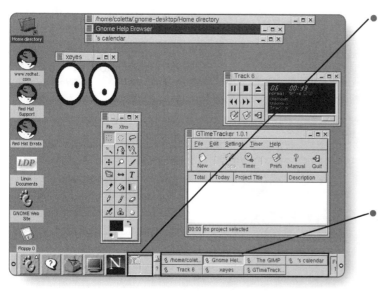

● **The Desktop view**. This view shows the number of desktop areas (which is like having separate monitor screens) available on the desktop. Each box within the desktop view is a desktop area. The desktop view also shows the arrangement of windows inside the desktop area.

● **Applications view**. The applications view displays all the icons representing open files and applications. If you can't find an application window, look at the icons and click on the one you need. The associated window will come to the front of the screen.

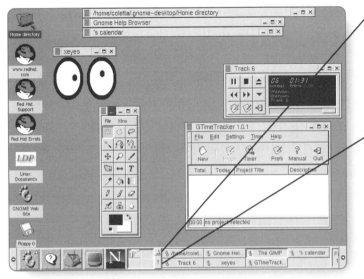

- **Task List**. The task list shows all the open applications. This list comes in handy when working with multiple applications on multiple desktop areas.

- **GNOME Pager settings**. With these settings you can change the number of pagers to display on your desktop as well as the settings for the task list.

Pushing Windows off a Desktop Area

Some people deal with cluttered desks by pushing things off, so try to push one of the windows off your desktop. The window will still be available, but it will be on a different desktop area.

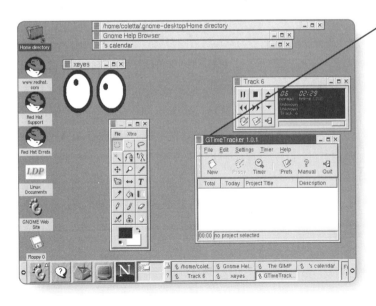

1. Click and **hold** on the **drag bar** of an open window on your desktop. The window will be selected.

2. Drag the **window** to the right. The window will move beyond the desktop area and part of the window will be hidden from sight.

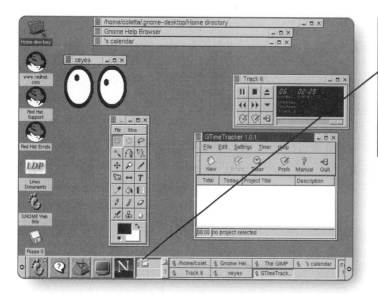

NOTE

If you watch the upper-left desktop area in the desktop view of the GNOME Pager, you'll see the window move.

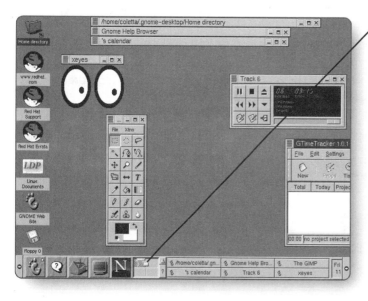

3. Click on the **upper-right desktop area** in the desktop view of the GNOME Pager. Another desktop area will appear and you'll see the part of the window that you moved off your original desktop area.

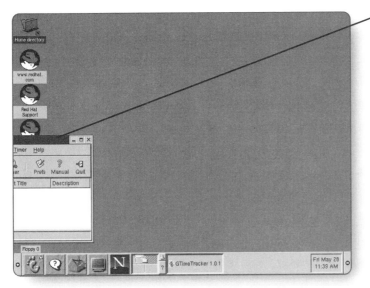

4. Click and **drag** the **application window** so that it is completely displayed in the second desktop area. The window will be open in the second desktop area on your screen.

Moving Between Desktop Areas

If you look at the GNOME pager on your panel, you'll see that one of the four rectangles in the Desktop view is highlighted to indicate the active desktop area. The small outline inside the highlighted rectangle represents the window you dragged with you.

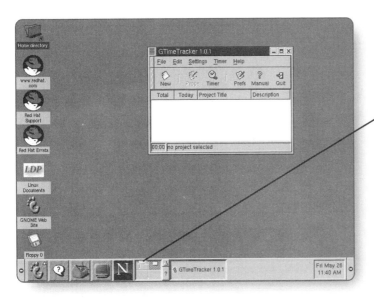

1. Click in the **upper-left desktop area** of the GNOME Pager to return to your original desktop. You move to that desktop but the window you dragged into the top-right desktop area will be left behind.

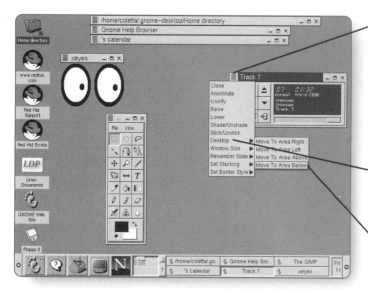

2. Click on the **Window Options Menu button** (located on the left side of the drag bar) of a window that you want to move to a different desktop area. The Window Options menu will appear.

3. Move the **mouse pointer** to Desktop. A second menu will appear.

4. Click on **one** of the four move options. The window will be moved to the selected desktop area.

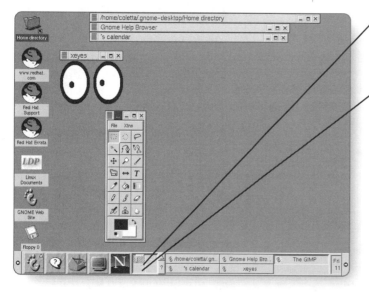

You'll notice that the window will appear in the desktop view for the selected desktop area.

5. Click on the **desktop area** where you just moved the application window. You will be able to work with the displayed application window.

Searching for Lost Applications

You could just start dragging things off your cluttered desktop area onto other desktop areas willy-nilly until you get to the bottom, but the GNOME pager can help you organize this easily.

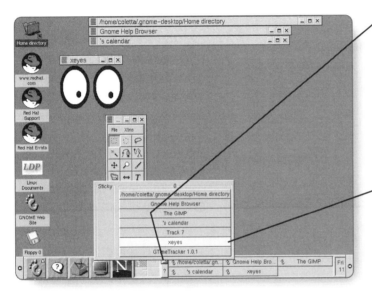

1. Click on the **Task List button** located in the center between the panes of the GNOME Pager. A menu will appear with buttons showing the titles of all the open applications on all the desktop areas.

2. Click on the **button** for the application window that you are having trouble locating. The GNOME Pager will search for the missing application window.

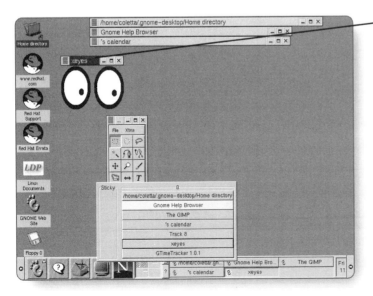

The application window will be selected and will appear at the top of the stack in your desktop area.

NOTE
If the application window you lost is located on another desktop area, you will be switched to that desktop area.

Creating Multiple Desktop Areas

Now you have a feel for dancing merrily through the four desktop areas that GNOME provides by default. You've also spent some time moving application windows between desktop areas, so now it's time to learn how to create even more desktop areas, or maybe fewer if you want a simpler desktop.

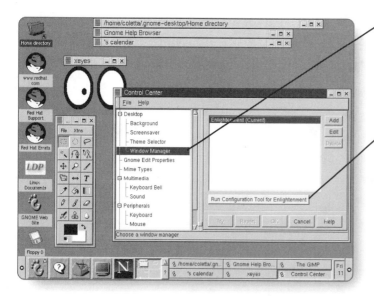

1. Click on the **GNOME Configuration Tool icon** on the panel. The GNOME Control Center will open.

2. Click on the **Window Manager option** in the left panel of the Control Center. The right pane will show the available window managers.

3. Click on the **Run Configuration Tool for Enlightenment button**. The Enlightenment Configuration Editor will open.

4. Click on the **Desktops option** in the upper-left of the configuration editor window. The Desktops pane will appear.

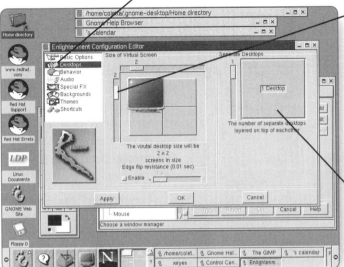

5. Click and **hold** on the **vertical slider** on the left side of the Virtual Screen and **drag** it **down**. The graphic changes to display more rows as you move the slider down; it displays fewer rows as the slider is moved up.

TIP

You can also create additional desktops. This is for more advanced users and network administrators to configure multiple discrete desktops.

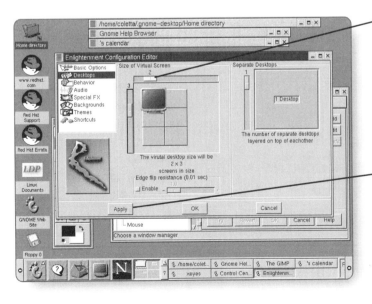

6. Click and **hold** on the **horizontal slider** and **drag** it to the **right**. The number of columns of desktop areas increases in the graphic. Moving the slider left decreases the number of columns.

7. Click on the **Apply button**. The GNOME Pager will change to show your setup for desktop areas.

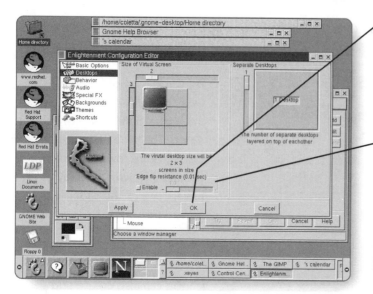

8. Click on **OK** when you are satisfied with your changes. You will return to the Control Center.

NOTE

The edge flip resistance slider controls the amount of delay in switching to a new desktop area when you move a window (using the mouse) from one desktop area to another.

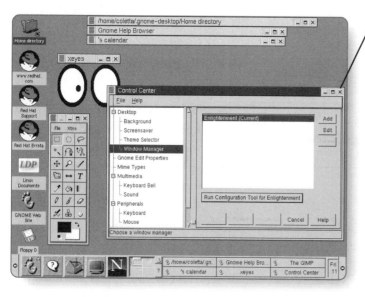

9. Click on the **Kill button**. The Control Center will close.

TIP

One way to organize desktop areas for your tasks is to assign each job to a desktop area of its own and simply click on the empty desktop area you want. If you forget where you put things, just look in the applications list on the pager.

4

Customizing the Screen Display

If you want to make your desktop more attractive, there are some cosmetic changes that you can make. For a little variety, change the picture or pattern that you use for a desktop background. To keep your screen from staying in one place for too long when you're not working, use a screen saver. There are many screen savers from which to choose and you can change settings if you need to slow down the motion. You can also change the appearance of window borders, mouse pointers, and dialog boxes. In this chapter, you'll learn how to:

- Create stylish desktop backgrounds
- Find some fun screen savers
- Use themes to change the look of window borders, mouse pointers, and dialog boxes.

Changing the Desktop Background

Whenever you're not looking at an application window, you'll probably see part of your desktop. You can really have some fun here, or you may opt for a background that makes it easier for you to see other screen elements such as windows and desktop icons. Browse through the selection of solid colors, gradients, and images.

Using a Solid Color Background

A solid color is the easiest background to create and the easiest on your eyes.

1. **Click** on the **GNOME Configuration Tool icon**. The Control Center will appear.

2. **Click** on the **Background option**. The Background pane will appear on the right side of the Control Center.

3. **Click** on the **Solid option button**. The option will be selected.

4. **Click** on the **Color 1 button**. The Pick a color dialog box will open.

5. Click on a **color** on the color wheel that matches the color you want to use as a background. The color will appear in the bar to the right of the color wheel.

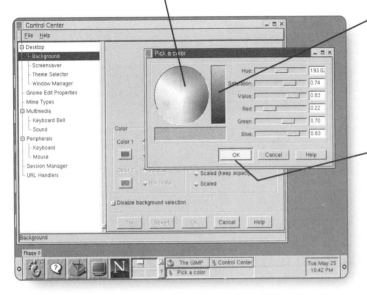

6. Click and **drag** the red **slider line**. Dragging the slider up will make the color lighter. Dragging the slider down will make the color darker. The color balance will change.

7. Click on **OK**. You will be returned to the Control Center and the color you selected will appear in the screen preview at the top of the Background pane.

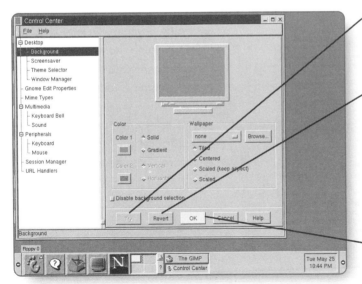

8. Click on the **Try button**. You'll see your background color appear on the desktop.

9. Click on the **Revert button** if you don't like the way the color matches the various screen elements. Your desktop background will change back to the original color. You can then try a different color.

10. Click on **OK** when you are satisfied with your color selection. Your changes will be applied and the background pane will disappear.

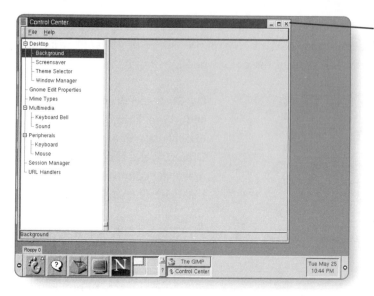

11. Click on the **Kill button**. The Control Center will close.

Creating a Gradient Background

A gradient is a combination of two colors. One color goes from darker to lighter and then blends with the second color, which also changes in brightness. If you're looking for a slightly psychedelic look that's also easy on the eyes, experiment with this background effect.

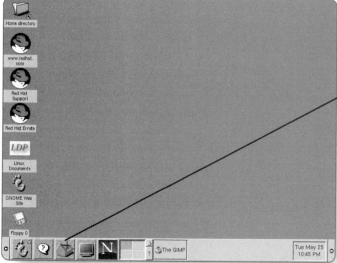

1. Click on the **GNOME Configuration Tool icon**. The Control Center will appear.

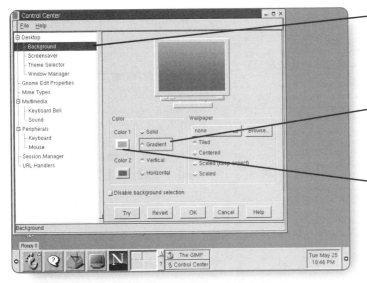

2. Click on the **Background option**. The Background pane will appear on the right side of the Control Center.

3. Click on the **Gradient option button**. The option will be selected.

4. Click on the **Color 1 button**. The Pick a color dialog box will open.

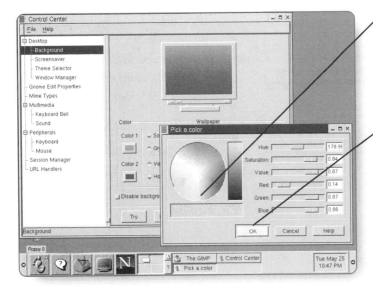

5. Click on a **color** that matches the color you want to use first. The color will appear in the two bars next to the color wheel.

6. Click on **OK**. You will return to the Control Center.

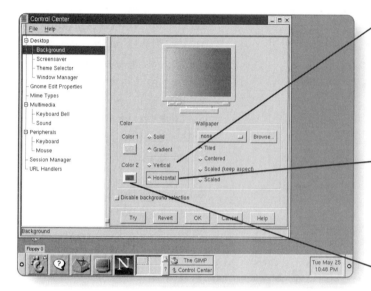

7a. Click on the **Vertical option button** if you want the gradient to go from side to side on your screen. The option will be selected.

OR

7b. Click on the **Horizontal option button** if you want the gradient to go from top to bottom. The option will be selected.

8. Click on the **Color 2 button**. The Pick a color dialog box will open.

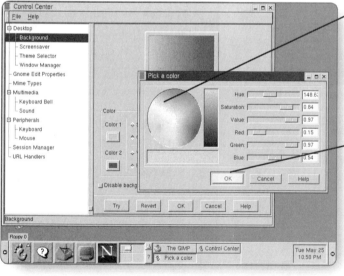

9. Click on a **color** on the color wheel that matches the color you want to use as the second color. The color will appear in the two bars next to the color wheel.

10. Click on **OK**. You will be returned to the Control Center.

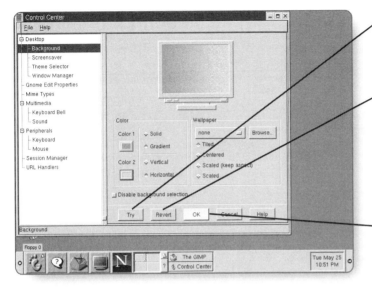

11. Click on the **Try button**. You'll see your background color appear on the desktop.

12. Click on the **Revert button** if you don't like the color selection. Your desktop background will change back to the original color. You can then try a different color.

13. Click on **OK** when you are satisfied with your color selection. Your changes will be applied.

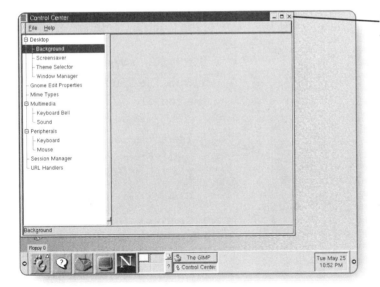

14. Click on the **Kill button**. The Control Center will close.

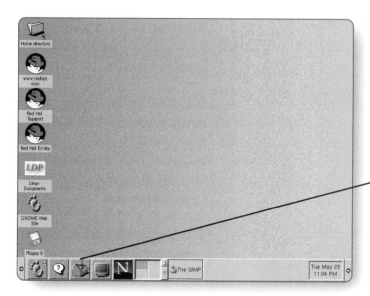

Selecting a Wallpaper

Linux comes loaded with a number of images that you can arrange in various ways to create a desktop wallpaper.

1. **Click** on the **GNOME Configuration Tool icon.** The Control Center will appear.

2. **Click** on the **Background option**. The Background pane will appear on the right side of the Control Center.

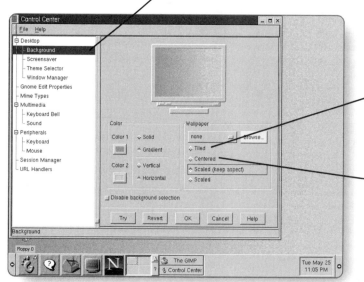

3. **Click** on a **Wallpaper option button**. The option will be selected.

- **Tiled**. This option tiles several copies of the image in rows and columns across the screen.

- **Centered.** This places one copy of the image in the center of the desktop. Any areas that are not used by the image will display the background color used.

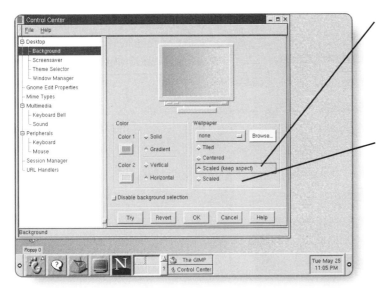

Scaled (keep aspect). This option stretches the image so that it takes up the majority of the desktop area but still keeps its original height and width proportions.

Scaled. Scaled fills the entire desktop with the image. The image may appear distorted.

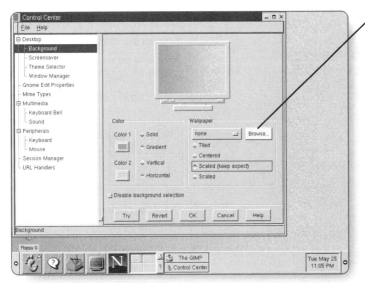

4. Click on the **Browse button**. The Wallpaper Selection dialog box will open.

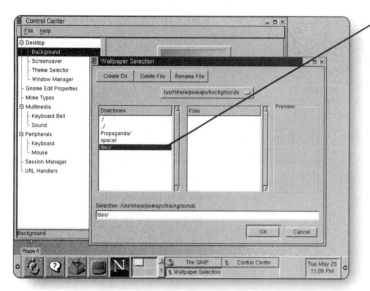

5. Double click on a **directory**. A list of files in that directory will appear in the Files list box.

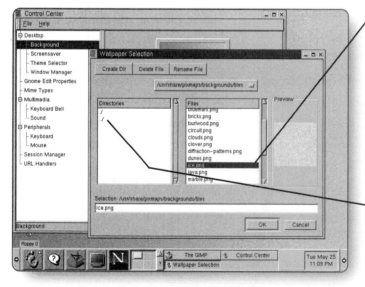

6. Click on a **file**. A preview of the background will appear in the Preview pane and the file name will appear in the Selection: text box.

7. Click on **another file** if you didn't like the first selection. The file will be selected.

8. Double-click on **../** to go back to the previous directory. The main list of wallpaper directories will appear.

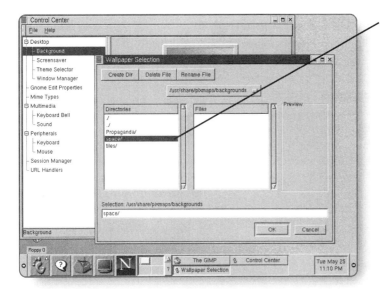

9. Double-click on the **directory** if you want to try another group of wallpapers.

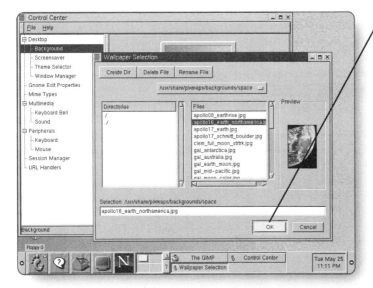

10. Click on **OK** when you have selected a wallpaper that you like. You will return to the Control Center.

11. Click on the **Try button**. You'll see a preview of the wallpaper in the preview screen at the top of the Control Center.

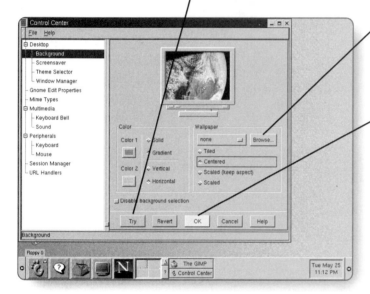

12. Click on the **Browse button** to try out other wallpapers if you are not satisfied.

13. Click on **OK**. Your changes will be applied and the Background pane will disappear.

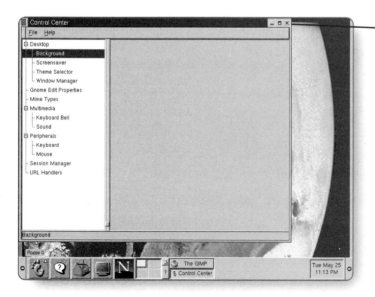

14. Click on the **Kill button**. The Control Center will close.

TIP

You can use the graphics applications (such as XPaint and The GIMP) that are installed in the Linux to create your own wallpaper.

Setting Up a Screen Saver

It's always a good idea to use a screen saver. You don't want a single static image to display for a long period of time on your screen. After a while, the image will appear "burned" into the monitor. This burned image will be there no matter what you are looking at. Screen savers change the image displayed on the monitor at a set speed. Screen savers also allow you to password-protect your desktop so that others can't use the computer while you are away.

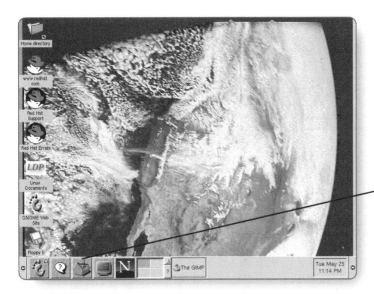

1. **Click** on the **GNOME Configuration Tool icon**. The Control Center will appear.

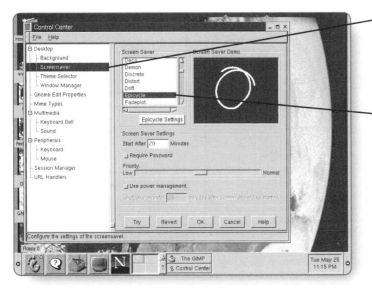

2. **Click** on **Screensaver**. The Screensaver pane will appear on the right side of the Control Center.

3. **Click** on a **screen saver**. The screen saver will be selected and you'll see a preview in the Screen Saver Demo section.

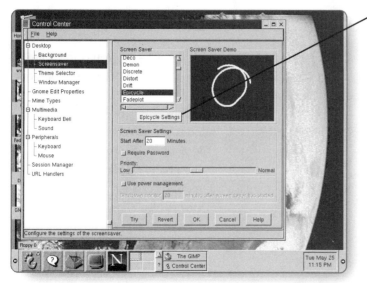

4. Click on the **Settings button** if you would like to change a setting such as speed, number of colors used, redraw rate, or number of pictures to use. The settings dialog box for the selected screen saver will appear.

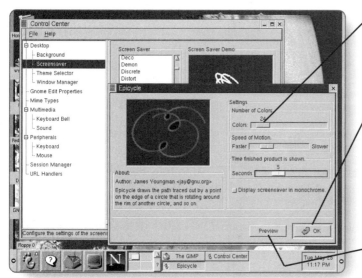

5. Click and **drag** the **sliders** to adjust the various settings for the screen saver. The settings will be changed.

6. Click on **OK**. The screen saver settings will be applied and you will return to the Control Center.

TIP

You can see the screen saver in action by clicking on the Preview button. To leave the screen saver and return to the Control Center, press the Escape key on your keyboard.

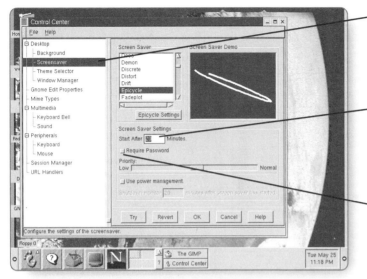

7. Double-click in the **Screen Saver Settings text box**. The default time setting will be selected.

8. Type the **number of minutes** of no activity on your computer after which you would like the screen saver to start.

9. Click on the **Require Password check button** if you want the screen saver password-protected. The option will be selected.

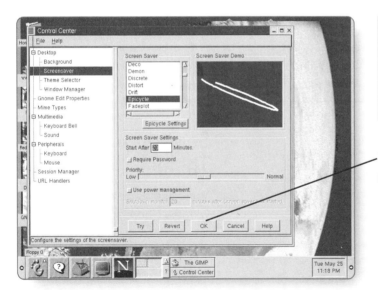

NOTE

Your screen saver uses your user account password.

10. Click on **OK**. The new screen saver will now be used.

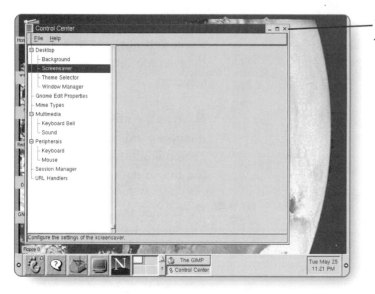

11. **Click** on the **Kill button**. The Control Center will close.

Working with Themes

There are a number of elements that you see when working with windows and dialog boxes that can be given a different look. If you find the default look difficult to see or too boring for your tastes, explore the various themes. There are a number of themes already included with Linux.

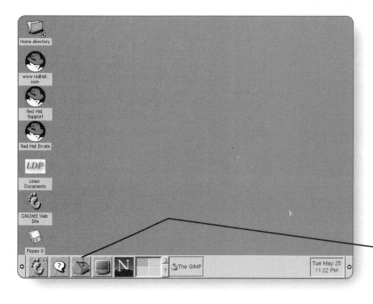

Selecting a Window Theme

You can change the look of a window's border and decorations using a number of installed themes in the Enlightenment Configuration Tool. These themes do not change anything located inside the window border.

1. **Click** on the **GNOME Configuration Tool icon**. The Control Center will appear.

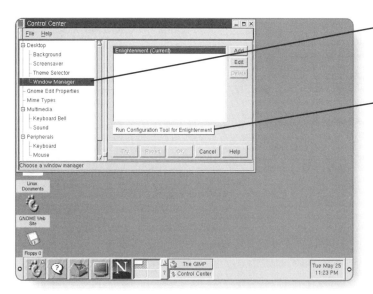

2. Click on the **Window Manager option**. The Window Manager pane will appear.

3. Click on the **Run Configuration Tool for Enlightenment button**. The Enlightenment Configuration Editor will appear.

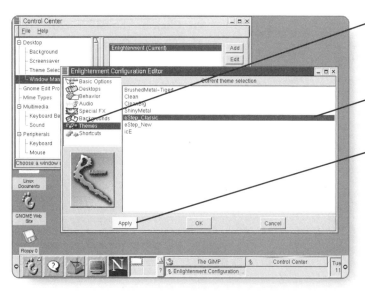

4. Click on the **Themes option**. The Current theme selection pane will appear.

5. Click on a **theme**. The theme will be selected.

6. Click on **Apply**. You'll see the new theme applied to all of the open windows on your desktop and to the mouse pointer.

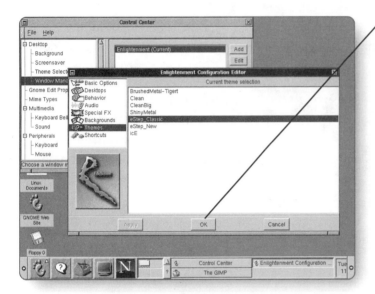

7. Click on **OK** when you have decided on a theme. You will return to the Control Center.

8. Click on the **Kill button**. The Control Center will close.

Choosing an Interface Theme

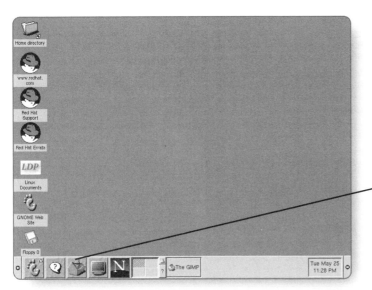

If you find the dialog boxes hard to work with, use one of the interface themes to give the dialog box elements a more familiar feel. Interface themes change the look of scroll bars, check buttons, and radio buttons.

1. **Click** on the **GNOME Configuration Tool icon**. The Control Center will appear.

2. **Click** on the **Theme Selector option**. The Theme Selector pane will appear on the right side of the Control Center.

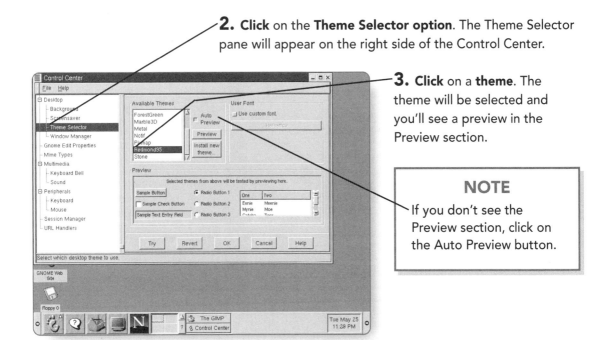

3. **Click** on a **theme**. The theme will be selected and you'll see a preview in the Preview section.

NOTE

If you don't see the Preview section, click on the Auto Preview button.

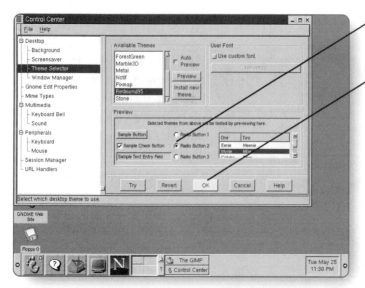

4. Click on an **element** to test how different elements function.

5. Click on **OK** when you find a theme that you like. Your changes will be applied.

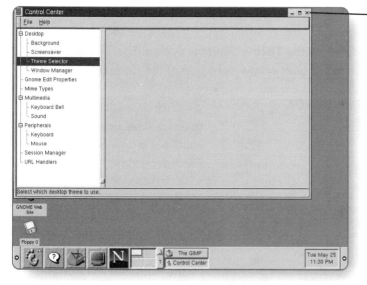

6. Click on the **Kill button**. The Control Center will close.

5

Managing Your Desktop

The Enlightenment Window Manager controls the appearance, behavior, background, and user interactions of windows. As you learned earlier, Enlightenment makes managing the virtual screen, configuring multiple desktops, and choosing themes and backgrounds a lot less complex. The GNOME interface adds more control and utilities to help you manage your desktop. GNOME allows you to create handy shortcuts to help you launch applications quicker. GNOME also helps you manage tasks and tools easily. In this chapter, you'll learn how to:

- Place applets on the GNOME Panel
- Use launchers to open applications and files
- Create drawers to store frequently accessed programs

Working with Applets on the GNOME Panel

There are already a number of applets on the GNOME Panel. The GNOME Pager is an applet and so is the clock. These applets are small applications that are available to assist you by performing various tasks or displaying important information. There are several applets from which you can choose. You'll find everything from amusements that provide a visual distraction to utilities for working with your computer's peripherals.

Entertaining from the GNOME Panel

There are a couple of fun games that you can keep permanently open on the GNOME Panel. They're small and unobtrusive, so maybe you won't find them so distracting.

1. **Right-click** on an **empty area** on the GNOME Panel. The Panel menu will appear.

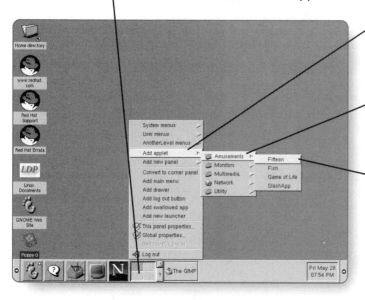

2. **Move** the **mouse pointer** to Add applet. The Applet menu will appear.

3. **Move** the **mouse pointer** to Amusements. The Amusements menu will appear.

4. **Click** on **Fifteen**. The icon for the Fifteen game will appear on the GNOME Panel.

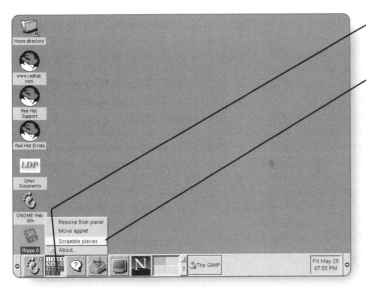

5. **Right–click** on the **Fifteen icon**. A menu will appear.

6. **Click** on **Scramble pieces**. The puzzle pieces will be mixed up and you can try and rearrange the individual squares so that they are in order.

Playing Your CDs

If you like to listen to music while you're working at your computer, keep a CD player on the GNOME Panel.

1. **Right-click** on an **empty area** on the GNOME Panel. The Panel menu will appear.

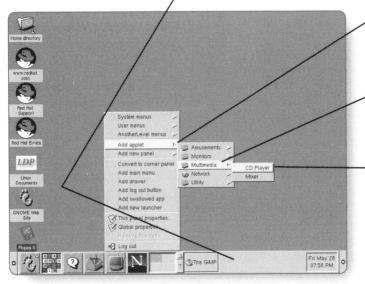

2. **Move** the **mouse pointer** to Add applet. The Applet menu will appear.

3. **Move** the **mouse pointer** to Multimedia. The Multimedia menu will appear.

4. **Click** on **CD Player**. The icon for the CD player will appear on the GNOME Panel.

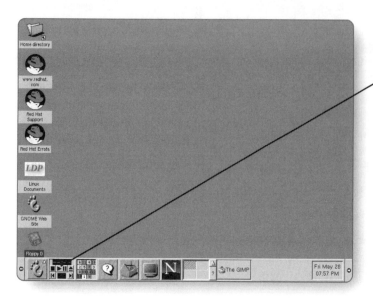

5. Place a **music CD** in your computer's CD-ROM drive.

6. Click on the **Play button** on the CD player. You should begin to hear music.

TIP

If you don't hear sound out of your speakers, Linux may need to be configured for your sound card. For help, point your Web browser to Red Hat's Web site. You may also want to check out www.opensound.com.

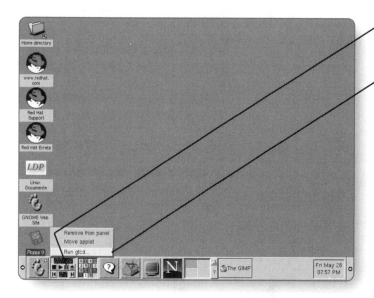

7. Right-click on the **CD player applet**. A menu will appear.

8. Click on **Run gtcd**. A more sophisticated CD player will appear on your screen.

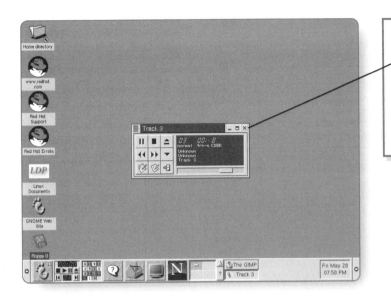

TIP

You can open and close this CD player without affecting the sound you hear from your computer speakers.

Moving Applets around on the GNOME Panel

You may not like where the applet was placed on the GNOME Panel by default. You can move any applet to any place on the GNOME Panel.

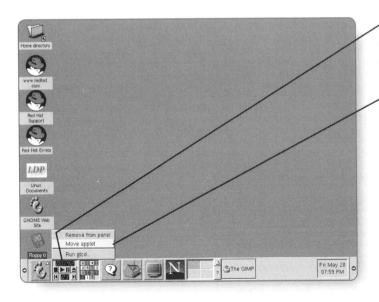

1. Right-click on the **applet** that you want to move. A menu will appear.

2. Click on **Move applet**. The applet will become a floating object on the GNOME Panel.

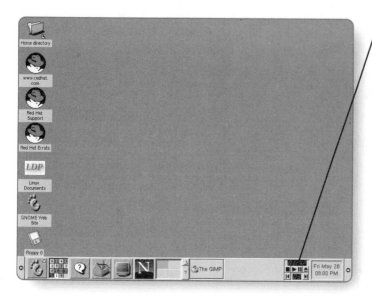

3. **Move** the **mouse pointer** to the place on the GNOME Panel where you want to move the applet. The applet will follow along with the mouse.

4. **Click** the **mouse button** when the applet is in the place where you want it. The applet will be positioned in the new spot.

Removing Applets from the GNOME Panel

You can also remove applets from the GNOME Panel.

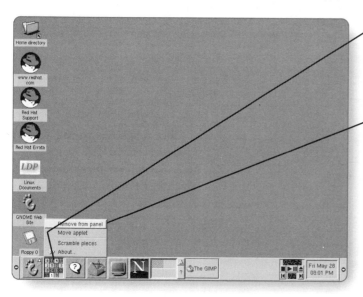

1. **Right-click** on the **applet** that you want to remove from the GNOME Panel. A menu will appear.

2. **Click** on **Remove from panel**. The applet will no longer appear on the GNOME Panel.

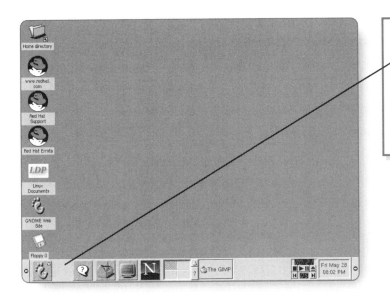

NOTE

If an empty space was left behind by the deleted applet, you can move the other icons to fill in the blank space.

Using Application Launchers

Application launchers are small icons that you place on the GNOME panel to start an application when you click on them. You can use these launchers to customize the panel and place all the tools and applications you need within easy reach.

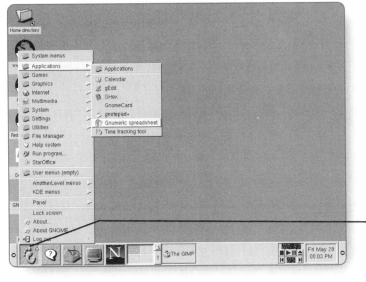

Adding a Launcher to the GNOME Panel

If the application or utility that you want to launch from the Panel is listed in the GNOME menu, use this quick method to place a launcher on the GNOME Panel.

1. Click on the **Main Menu Button**. The Main Menu will appear.

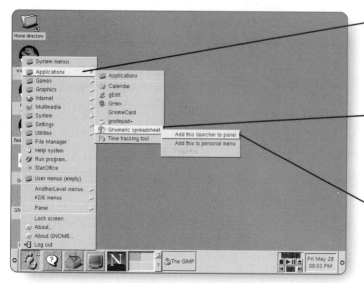

2. Display the **menu** that contains the application that you want to place on the GNOME Panel. The menu will appear.

3. Right-click on the **application** or **utility** you want to launch from the GNOME Panel. A menu will appear.

4. Click on **Add this launcher to panel**. A launcher icon will appear on the panel.

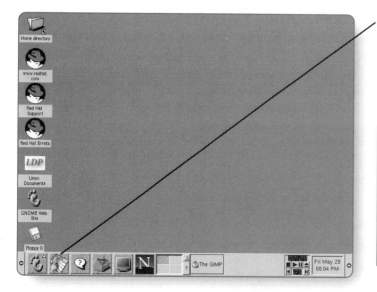

Instead of wading through the menus to start frequently used applications, just click on the launcher and the application will start.

NOTE

If you don't like where the launcher is placed, you can move it to a different place on the GNOME Panel.

Changing the Launcher Icon

Each application has a default launcher icon. If you want something different, there are many different icons from which you can choose.

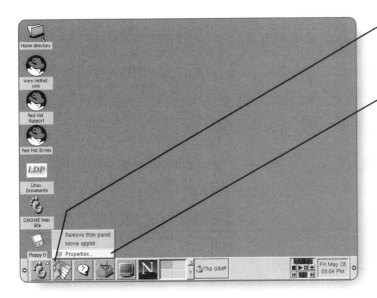

1. Right-click on the **launcher icon** you want to change. A menu will appear.

2. Click on **Properties**. The Launcher properties dialog box will appear.

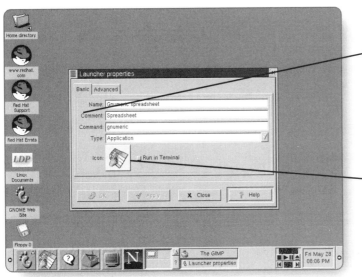

TIP

To change the tool tip that appears when the mouse is held over the launcher icon, edit the text in the Comment: text box.

3. Click on the **Icon button**. The Choose an icon dialog box will open.

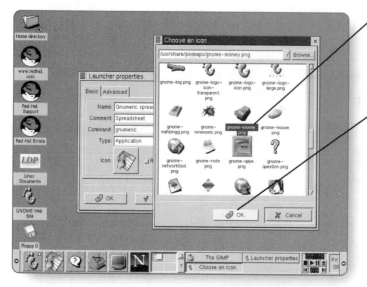

4. Click on the **icon** that you want to use from the list of thumbnails. The icon will be selected.

5. Click on **OK**. You'll return to the Launcher properties dialog box and the icon you selected will appear on the Icon button.

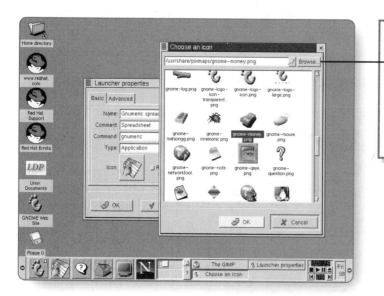

TIP

If you have a picture stored on your computer that you want to use for the icon, click on the browse button to find it.

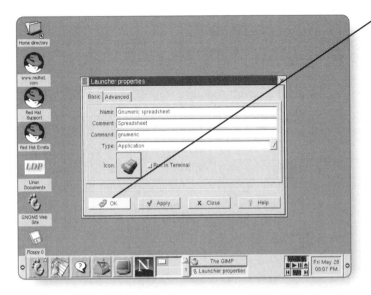

6. Click on **OK**. The picture used for the launcher icon changes on the GNOME Panel.

Deleting Launchers

You can delete unused or unnecessary launchers from the Panel with a few mouse clicks.

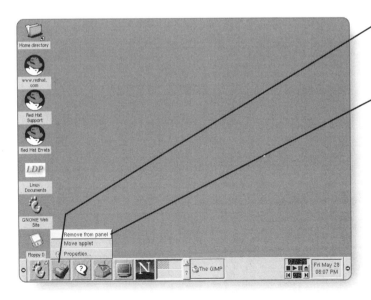

1. Right-click on the **launcher icon** that you want to delete. A menu will appear.

2. Click on **Remove from panel**. The launcher will disappear from your GNOME Panel.

Adding Drawers to the GNOME Panel

Drawers are small pop-up menus of launcher icons that sit as a button on the Panel. You may use them to keep all the applications associated with a particular job together or you may even select a whole menu of items from the GNOME menus and place it on the Panel as a drawer.

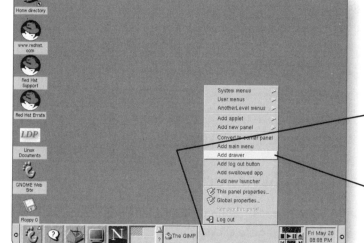

Creating the Drawer

1. Right-click on an **empty area** of the GNOME Panel. The Panel menu will appear.

2. Click on **Add drawer**. A drawer icon will appear on the GNOME Panel.

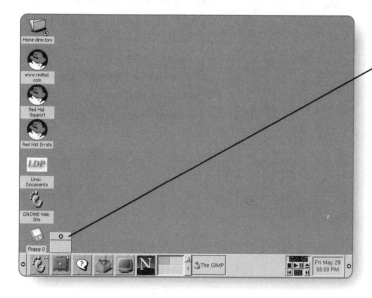

NOTE

The drawer is open and empty. To close the drawer, you can either click on the icon on the GNOME Panel or click on the down arrow at the top of the open drawer.

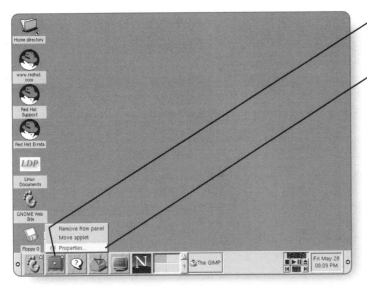

3. Right-click on the **drawer icon**. A menu will appear.

4. Click on **Properties**. The Panel properties dialog box will open and the Drawer tab will be at the top of the stack.

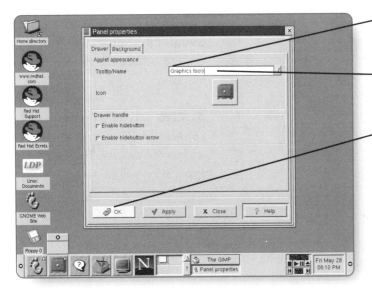

5. Click in the **Tooltip/Name text box.**

6. Type a **name** you want to use to identify the drawer.

7. Click on **OK**. The dialog box will close. When you hold the cursor over the new drawer, the tooltip name appears.

NOTE

You can move the drawer to any spot on the GNOME Panel.

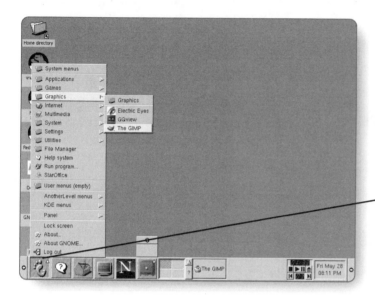

Filling up the Drawer

Now you'll need to add some things to the new drawer. Before you begin adding items to the drawer, you'll want to make sure the drawer is open.

1. Click on the **Main Menu Button**. The main menu will appear.

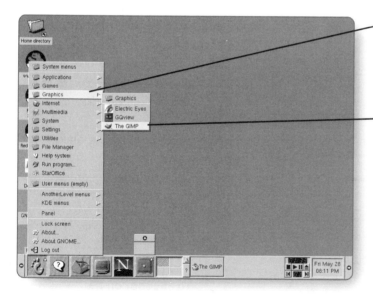

2. Display the **menu** that contains the application that you want to add to the drawer. The menu will appear.

3. Click and **hold** on the **application** that you want to add to the drawer. The application will be selected.

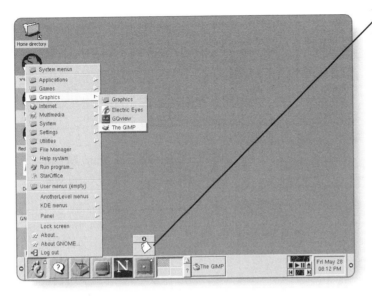

4. Drag the **mouse pointer** so that it is over the open drawer. The drawer will be highlighted.

5. Release the **mouse button**. The launcher icon for the selected application will appear on the drawer tab.

NOTE

If the Main Menu or any of its submenus are covering the drawer tab, you must move the drawer before you can place the application in the drawer.

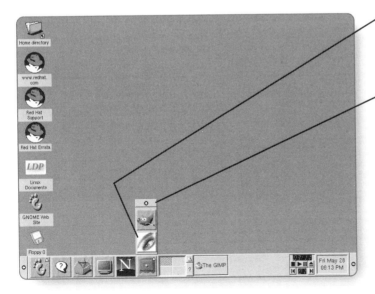

6. Drag more **applications** from the menu to the drawer and watch the icons line up.

7. Click on the **down arrow** on the drawer tab or on the drawer icon. The drawer will close.

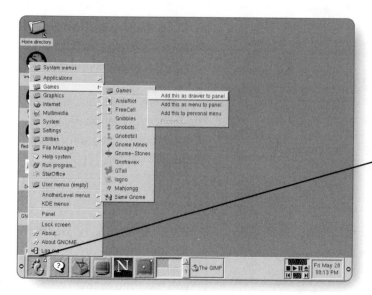

Creating a Drawer from the Main Menu

You can make an entire submenu from the GNOME menu into a drawer.

1. **Click** on the **Main Menu button**. The Main Menu will appear.

2. **Display** the **menu** that you want to turn into a drawer on the GNOME Panel. The menu will appear.

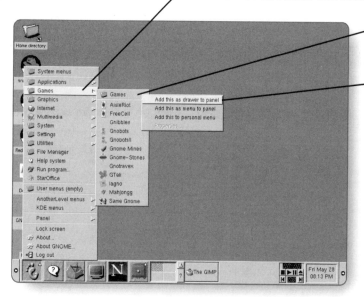

3. **Right-click** on the **menu title bar**. A menu will appear.

4. **Click** on **Add this as drawer to panel**. The drawer and all of the contents of the menu will be placed on the GNOME Panel.

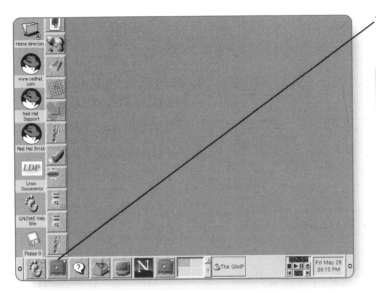

The menu contents will become icons on the drawer tab.

Changing Launcher and Drawer Icon Backgrounds

You'll notice that each of the icons on the GNOME Panel contains a picture on top of a gray textured background. You can change this background.

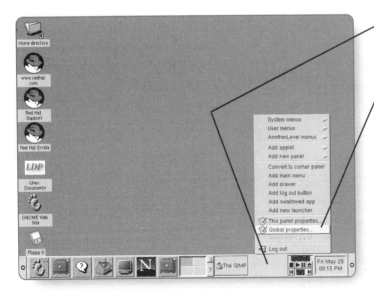

1. Right-click on an **empty area** of the GNOME Panel. A menu will appear.

2. Click on **Global properties**. The Global panel configuration dialog box will open.

3. Click on either the **Launcher icon** or **Drawer icon tab**. The tab will come to the top of the stack.

4. Click on the **Tile filename (up) button**. The Browse dialog box will open.

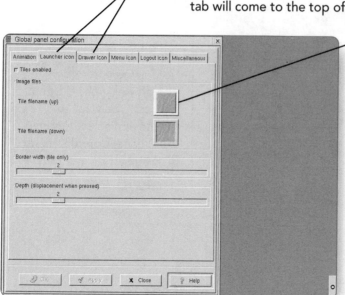

5. Click on a **tile icon** in the list. The tile will be selected.

6. Click on **OK**. You'll be returned to the Global panel configuration dialog box and you'll see the tile you just selected in the Tile filename (up) button.

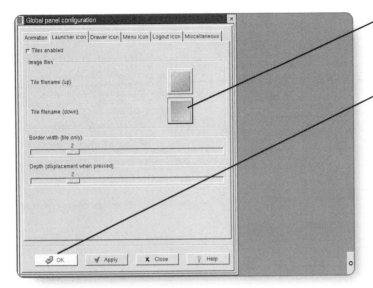

7. Change the **tile** for the Tile filename (down) button. The tile color will be changed.

8. Click on **OK**. The icon backgrounds will be changed.

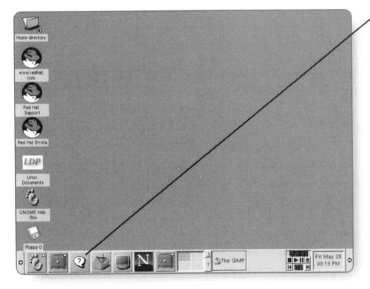

Notice the different background. Experiment with backgrounds for different icons until you come up with a scheme that you like.

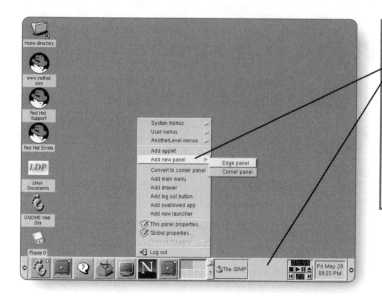

TIP

If you begin to run out of space on the GNOME Panel, you can always add another panel. Right click on an empty area of the GNOME Panel and select Add new panel from the menu that appears.

Part I Review Questions

1. Why is it so important to create user accounts and not work in the root account? *See "Starting Linux for the First Time" in Chapter 1*

2. What are the basic elements of the GNOME user interface? *See "Exploring GNOME" in Chapter 1*

3. How do you open an application in GNOME? *See "Opening Program Windows" in Chapter 2*

4. Name two different methods you can use to change the size of a window. *See "Resizing a Window" in Chapter 2*

5. Can GNOME automatically arrange the multiple open windows on your desktop for you? *See "Working with Multiple Windows" in Chapter 3*

6. How do you navigate multiple desktop areas with the GNOME Pager? *See "Working with Multiple Desktop Areas" in Chapter 3*

7. What kinds of backgrounds can you put on your desktop? *See "Changing the Desktop Background" in Chapter 4*

8. Where do you find the screen savers available to you? *See "Setting Up a Screen Saver" in Chapter 4*

9. How do you place an applet on the GNOME Panel? *See "Working with Applets on the GNOME Panel" in Chapter 5*

10. Why would you want to put drawers on the GNOME Panel? *See "Adding Drawers to the GNOME Panel" in Chapter 5*

PART II

Using the File System

6

Exploring the File System

It's time to take a look at one place in the Linux operating system in which you'll be spending a lot of time—the file system. You'll be using the GNOME File Manager to create directories and manage files. The applications also use the file system to save and access files that were created or modified. If you've never used Linux or Unix before, you'll find that the GNOME File Manager uses a filing system that is different from what you may have used with other operating systems. In this chapter, you'll learn how to:

- Identify the basic parts of the file manager
- Navigate the directory structure
- Select files in the directory structure
- Sort through your file list

Opening the File System

Before you start working with applications and creating files, take some time to get familiar with the Linux file system. You'll perform most of your file maintenance tasks from the file manager, which is an easy-to-use graphical filing system.

1. Double-click on the **Home directory desktop icon**. The GNOME File Manager will open. When the File Manager opens, your user directory will be selected.

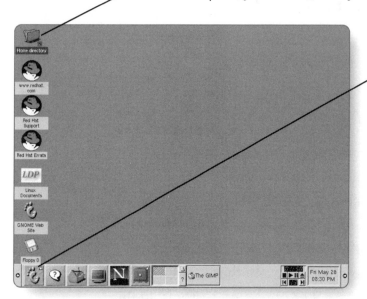

NOTE

If you don't see the Home directory desktop icon, open the Main Menu button and click on File Manager.

Looking at File Manager

The GNOME File Manager is the graphical interface in which you'll perform all of your filing tasks. You may find similarities between this file manager and file managers used with other operating systems.

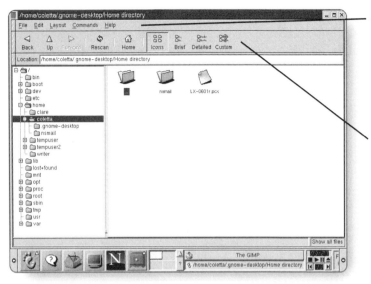

● The menus contain all of the commands you can perform with the file manager. You can create directories, delete files, sort files, and view directories.

● The toolbar makes it easy to navigate the file system and change how you view your files and directories.

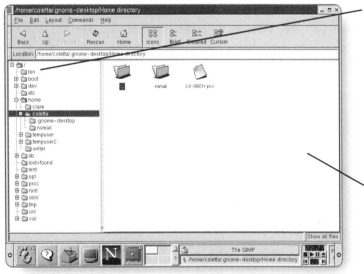

● The tree view is located in the left pane and shows all of the directories on your Linux system. When you open the file manager, your home user directory is selected by default. This is the main directory where you will store your user files and folders.

● The directory view is located in the right pane and shows all the files and subdirectories stored in the directory selected in the tree view.

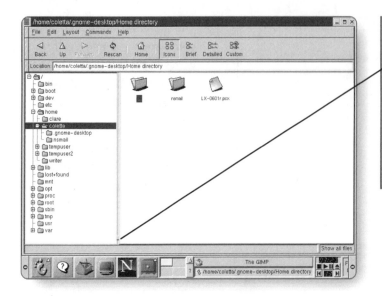

TIP

You can change the size of the tree view and directory view panes. Click and drag the resize box located at the bottom of the bar between the two panes.

Understanding the Linux File System

Before you dive into the Linux file system, you need to understand the contents of the directory structure that was set up when you installed your Linux. Some of these directories contain information that you'll find useful. Other directories are best left alone unless you are a Linux expert.

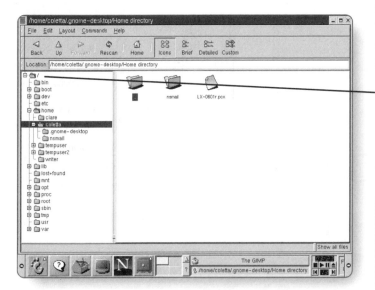

- The / or root directory is the base of the Linux file system. All of the files and directories for the system are contained in this directory.

TIP

Do not store any of your files in the root directory!

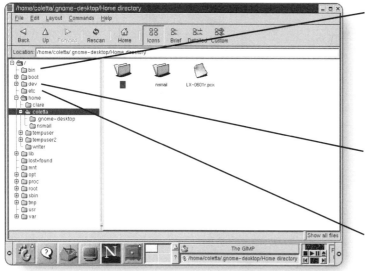

- The /bin directory holds the basic Linux programs and commands. You probably won't need to use this directory. The GNOME interface accesses many of these programs and commands for you.

- The /dev directory is where all of the device files for each hardware component on your computer are stored.

- The /etc directory contains system configuration files and initialization scripts.

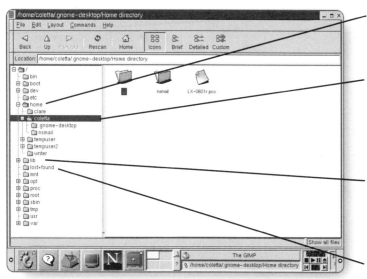

- The /home directory contains directories for all the user accounts on the system.

- Each user has a home directory in which to store personal files. You cannot access another user's files from your user account.

- The /lib directory is where the library files for C and other programming languages are stored.

- If Linux has lost a file, it might be found in the /lost+found directory.

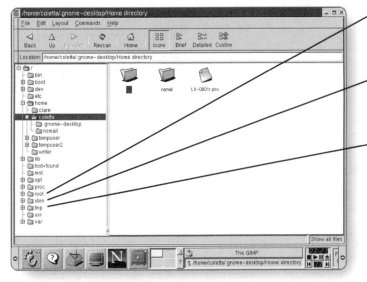

• The home directory for the superuser or root account is /root.

• The /sbin directory contains a number of tools used for system administration.

• The /tmp directory is where all users can store files on a temporary basis. If the system is rebooted, all files in the tmp directory will be lost.

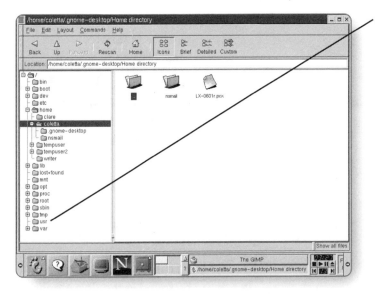

• The /usr directory contains a number of Linux commands and utilities that are not a part of the Linux operating system, documentation files and some utility programs, and the Linux game collection.

Browsing the File System

The graphical interface used by the file manager makes it easy to move around and view the contents of the various directories. Because you don't have any directories created in your user account, the safest place to play in the file system is the /usr directory.

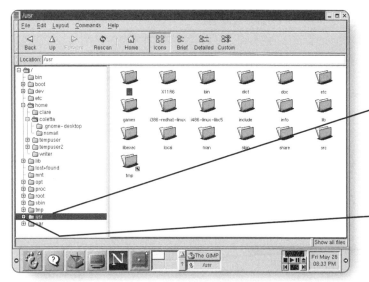

1. Click on the **/usr directory** in the tree view. The list of subdirectories and files contained in the /usr directory will appear in the directory view.

2. Click on the **plus sign** next to the /usr directory. The list of subdirectories will appear under the /usr directory in the tree view.

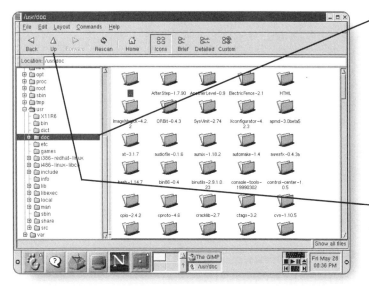

3. Click on the **plus sign** next to the /usr/man directory. The directory in the tree view will expand and the list of directories and files contained in the /usr/man directory will appear in the directory view.

NOTE

To move to the directory one level up from the selected directory, click on the Up button on the toolbar.

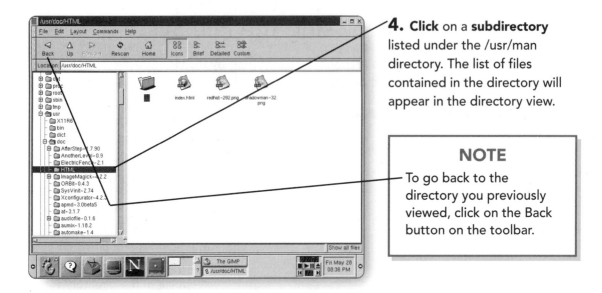

4. Click on a **subdirectory** listed under the /usr/man directory. The list of files contained in the directory will appear in the directory view.

NOTE

To go back to the directory you previously viewed, click on the Back button on the toolbar.

5. Click on each of the **view buttons**. You will be able to view the contents of a directory in three different ways.

● **The Icons view** shows a picture that represents the file type and the name of the file underneath. This is useful if you're looking for a quick way to determine file types.

● **The Brief view** provides a simple list of the files stored in the directory.

TIP

To change the size of the directory view columns, click and drag the edge of the column heading.

• **The Detailed view** gives information about the file size and when it was last used. This view allows you to sort the list in a number of ways.

Selecting Files

Before you can perform a task on a file (such as copy or rename), you'll need to select the file in the file manager. You have the choice of selecting files yourself by clicking on the files with the mouse or telling the file manager the types of files you want to select and it will search the directory and select those files for you.

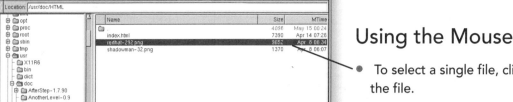

Using the Mouse

• To select a single file, click on the file.

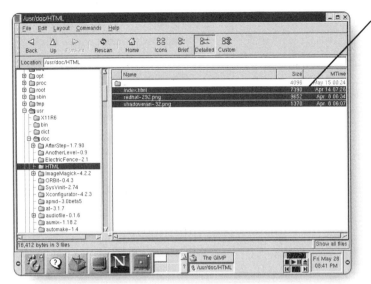

● To select several contiguous files, click on the first file that you want to select, then press the Shift key and click on the last file you want to select.

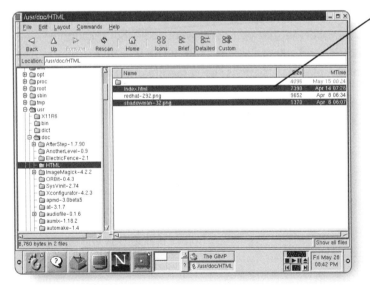

● To select files that are not located next to each other, press and hold the Ctrl key while you click on each file that you want to select.

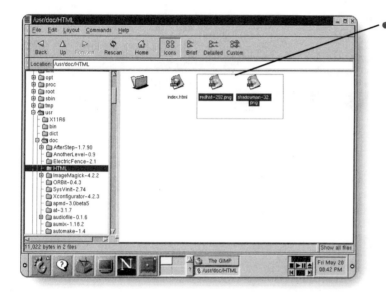

● To select several contiguous files in the Icons view, click and hold the mouse button at the beginning of one file, then drag the mouse to the end of the last file you want to select.

Using Selection Criteria

You may decide that you don't want to search through a directory and select files yourself. If the files all contain a common element, such as the same file extension, or the files begin with the same combination of letters, you can use the sort filter.

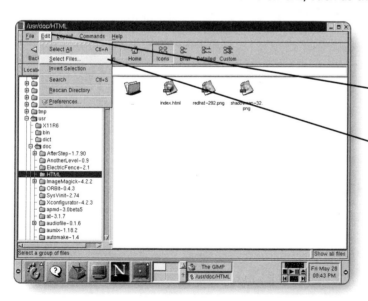

1. Click on **Edit**. The Edit menu will appear.

2. Click on **Select Files**. The Select dialog box will open.

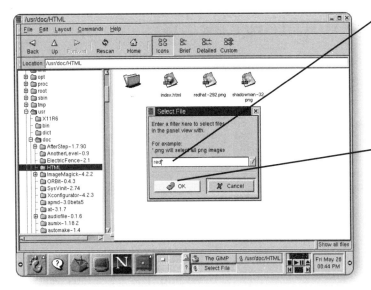

3. Type the **criteria** for the files you want to select. For example, if you want to find all files that use the "pcx" file extension, type *.pcx. If you want to select files starting with "LX," type LX*.

4. Click on **OK**. The filter will search for those files that match the criteria you typed.

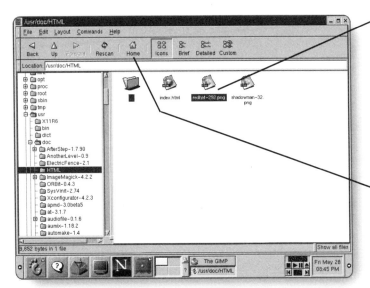

All of the files that matched the criteria will be selected in the file manager window. You may need to scroll down the directory view pane to see highlighted files.

TIP

When you are finished looking through the /usr directory and want to go back to your user account directory, click on the Home button.

Sorting the File List

You can sort the list of files in the detailed view by file name, file size, and date last accessed.

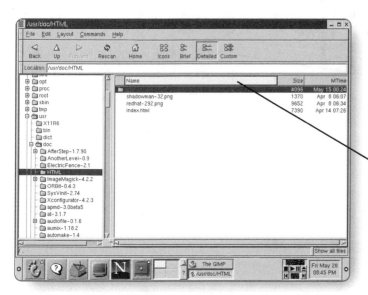

Reordering the File List

The column headings at the top of the directory view allow you to sort your files quickly.

1. Click on the **Name column heading**. The list of files will be sorted by name, with files beginning with Z at the top of the list and those starting with A at the bottom.

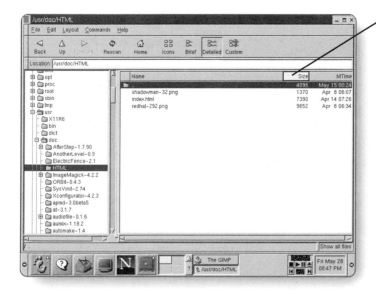

2. Click on the **Size column heading**. The list of files will be sorted by size from the smallest file size down to the largest file size.

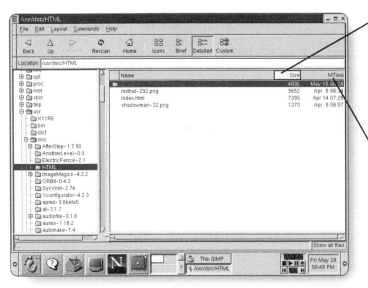

3. Click on the **Size column heading** a second time. The list of files will be sorted from the largest file size down to the smallest file size.

NOTE

You can also sort files by the date they were last used by clicking on the MTime column heading.

Filtering the Files List

You may decide that you only want to see certain files listed in the directory view. Here's how you can hide those files that you don't need to view.

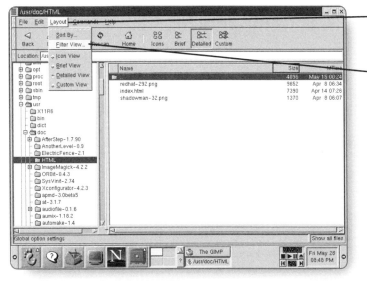

1. Click on **Layout**. The Layout menu will appear.

2. Click on **Filter View**. The Set Filter dialog box will open.

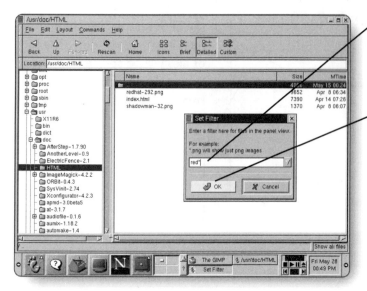

3. Click in the **text box** and **type** the **criteria** for the files that you want to display in the file list.

4. Click on **OK**. The filter will search for those files that match the criteria you typed. Only those files that fit the selected criteria will display.

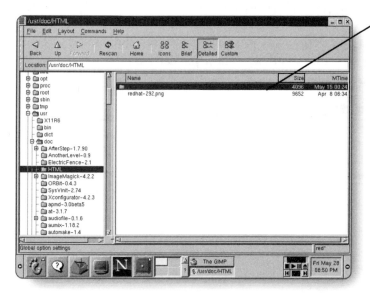

If you filtered a file list and want to see the entire contents, you will need to remove the filter.

5. Click on **Layout**. The Layout menu will appear.

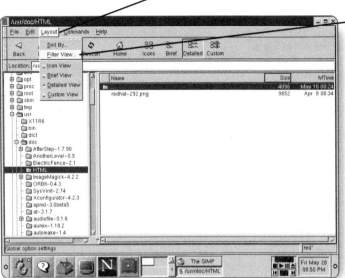

6. Click on **Filter View**. The Set Filter dialog box will open.

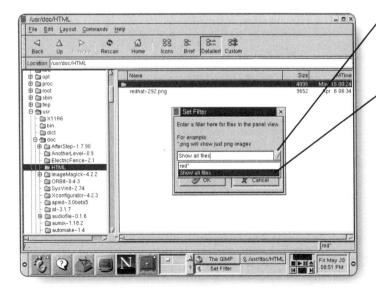

7. Click on the **down arrow** to the right of the text box. A drop-down list will appear.

8. Click on **Show all files**. The option will be selected.

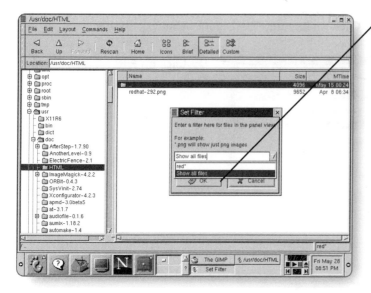

9. Click on **OK**. The entire list of files contained in the directory will appear in the directory view.

7

Organizing the File System

During the Linux installation you set up a superuser (or root) account inside your Linux system, and one or more user accounts along the way. When you log in to your user account and open the file manager, the home directory for your account is already selected. This is the only directory on the Linux system where you have permission to store your files. Once you build a personal filing system, you can begin to move your files around. In this chapter, you'll learn how to:

- Create a new directory
- Move and copy files
- Rename and delete files and directories
- Search for misplaced files in your home directory
- Move frequently-used files to your desktop

Creating Directories

When you create a file in an application, you'll need to save it to the Linux file system. You could place all the files in the home directory, but things might get cluttered after a while. The first task is to create a few directories in which to categorize your work. For example, create a folder for each type of document—word processing, spreadsheet, graphics—or for a small business, set up a separate folder for each client or project.

1. **Double-click** on the **Home button**. The home directory for your user account will be selected in the tree view.

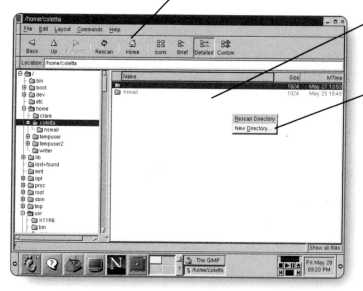

2. **Right-click** on an **empty area** of the directory view. A menu will appear.

3. **Click** on **New Directory**. The Create a New Directory dialog box will appear.

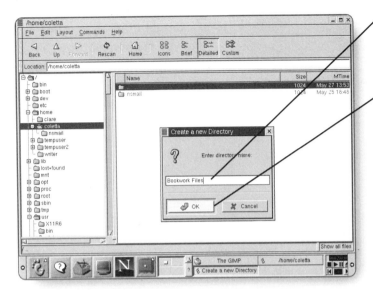

4. Type a **name** for the directory in the Enter directory name: text box.

5. Click on **OK**. The new directory will appear in the directory view.

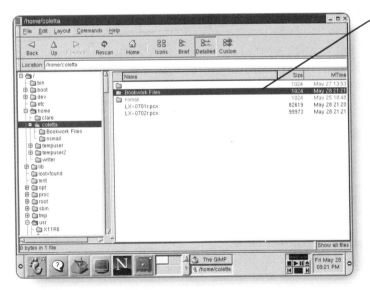

6. Double-click on the new **directory** in the directory view. The folder will be added to your user account in the tree view and the directory view will be empty.

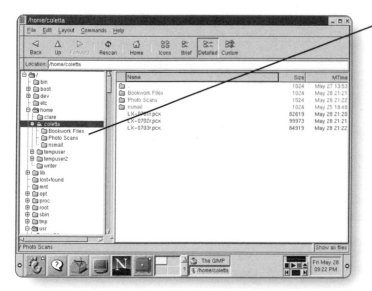

7. **Create** other **directories** that you might need. You can make more directories under your home directory, or make subdirectories within directories to further organize your files.

Copying and Moving Files

If you've used any Linux applications and created a file, the default location where the file was saved was your home directory. You can copy or move these files into directories that you've created under your home directory. This will make it easier to keep your filing system organized. You'll learn how to create files in Chapter 10, "Working with Files."

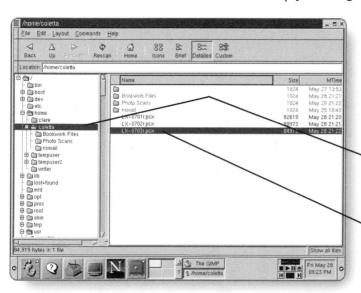

Using Drag and Drop

The easiest way to copy and move files is with the mouse.

1. Display the **destination directory** in the tree view. It will be displayed.

2. Click and **hold** on the **file** that you want to copy. The file will be selected.

3. **Drag** the **mouse pointer** to the directory to which you want to copy the file. The directory will be selected.

4. **Release** the **mouse button**. The file will be copied to the destination directory.

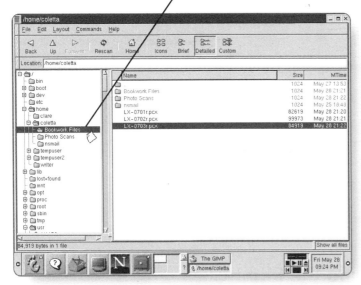

You can also use the drag-and-drop method to move a file to another directory.

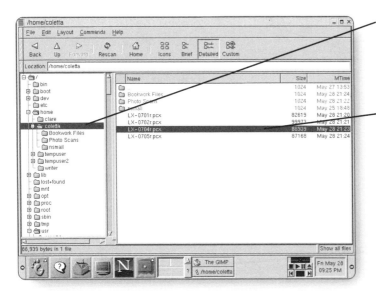

5. **Display** the **destination directory** in the tree view. The destination directory for the file will be displayed.

6. **Press** the **Shift key** and **click and hold** on a **file**. The file will be selected.

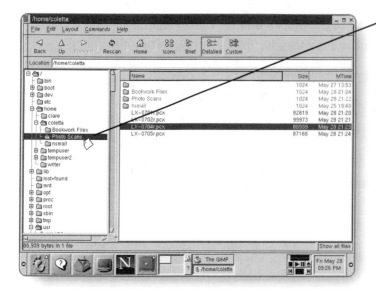

7. Move the **mouse pointer** to the destination directory. The directory will be selected.

8. **Release** the **mouse button**. The file will be moved.

Using the Right-Click

If you just can't get the hang of those drag-and-drop dance steps, you can also move and copy files using a menu.

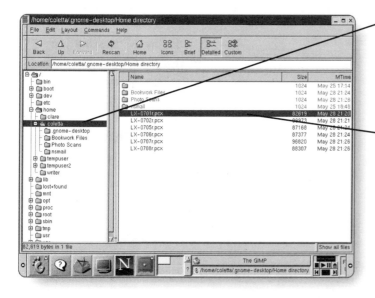

1. **Open** the **directory** that contains the file that you want to move or copy. The list of files contained in the directory will appear in the directory view.

2. **Right-click** on the **file** that you want to copy or move. A menu will appear.

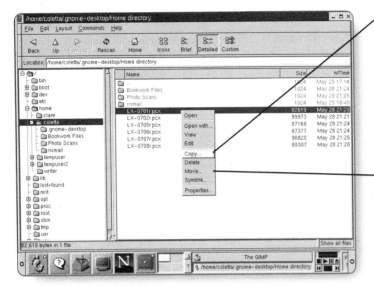

3a. Click on **Copy** if you want to make a copy of the file to place in another directory. The Copy dialog box will open and the Destination tab will be at the top of the stack.

OR

3b. Click on **Move** if you want to move the file to a different directory. The Move dialog box will open and the Destination tab will be at the top of the stack.

NOTE

The Copy and Move dialog boxes work the same way.

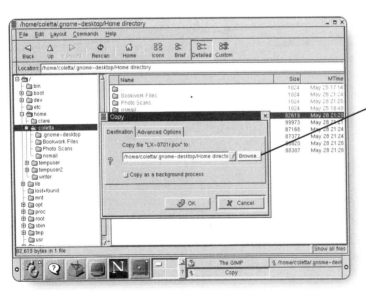

4. Click on the **Browse button**. The Find Destination Folder dialog box will open.

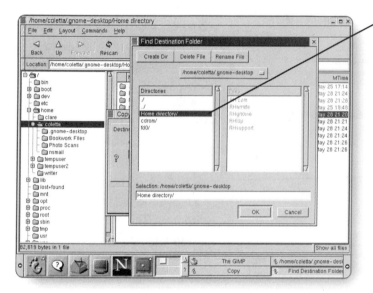

5. Double-click on your **home directory** in the Directories list. The list of directories in your user account will appear.

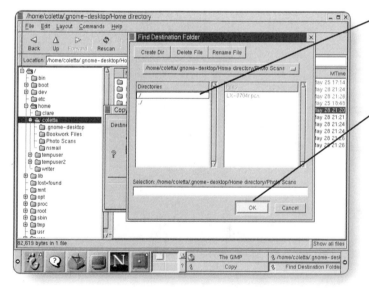

6. Click on the **directory** into which you want to move or copy the file. The directory will be selected.

7. Click on **OK**. The directory path will appear in the Copy file or Move file text boxes.

TIP

If you know the directory path, you can type it in the Copy file or Move file text box.

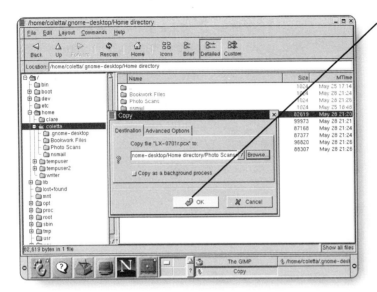

8. Click on **OK**. The file will be copied or moved to the selected directory.

Renaming Files

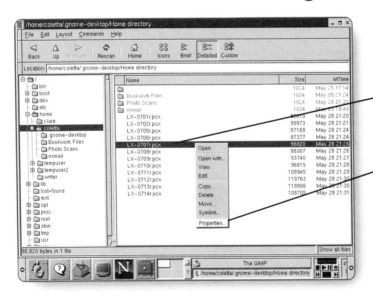

You may decide to rename a file. You can easily change the name of a file.

1. Right-click on the **file** that you want to rename. A menu will appear.

2. Click on **Properties**. The properties dialog box for the file will open.

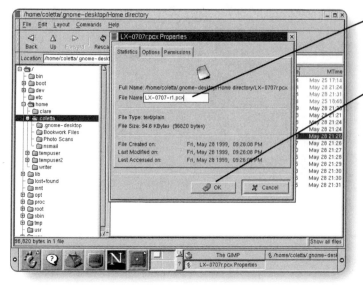

3. **Click** in the **File Name text box** and **type** a new **name** for the file.

4. **Click** on **OK**. The file will be renamed.

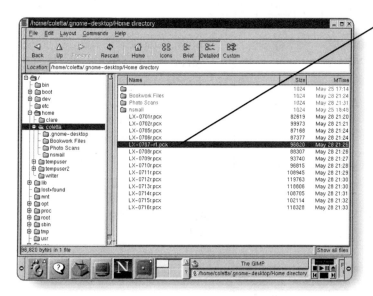

The new file name will appear in the directory view.

TIP

You can change a directory name by displaying the directory in the directory view, right-clicking on the directory, and selecting Properties from the menu that appears.

Removing Files and Directories

You may decide to delete some files and directories in your home directory. Before you can delete a directory, you'll first need to delete all the files from the directory.

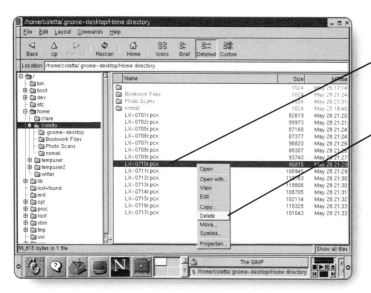

Deleting Files

1. Right-click on the **file** that you want to delete. A menu will appear.

2. Click on **Delete**. A confirmation dialog box will open.

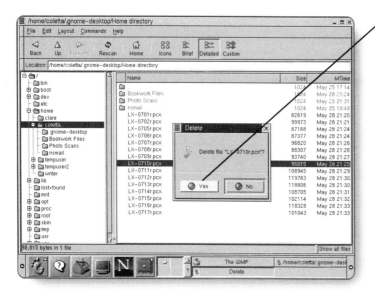

3. Click on **Yes**. The file will be deleted.

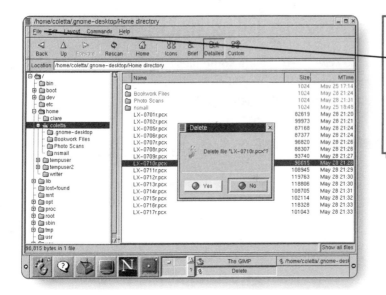

NOTE

If you can't get the right-click menu, click on the File menu to find the commands for copying, moving, and deleting files.

Working with Confirmation Dialog Boxes

To delete files, a confirmation box will ask if you want to perform the specified action. You can change the file manager so that dialog boxes no longer appear. You may want to wait until you are comfortable with Linux before you do this.

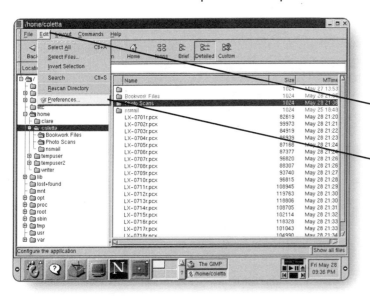

1. **Click** on **Edit**. The Edit menu will appear.

2. **Click** on **Preferences**. The Preferences dialog box will open and the File display tab will be at the top of the stack.

3. **Click** on the **Confirmation tab**. The Confirmation tab will come to the top of the stack.

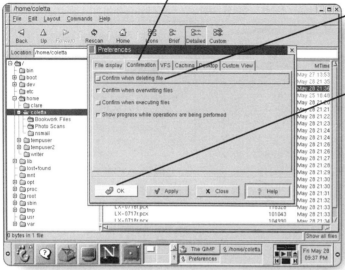

4. **Click** on the **Confirm when deleting file check button**. The option will be deselected.

5. **Click** on **OK**. The confirmation box will no longer display.

Finding Files in Your Home Directory

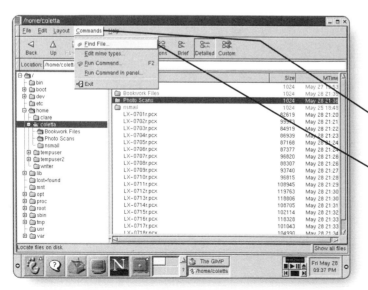

After moving and copying files all over your home directory, you may have some trouble trying to find a specific file.

1. **Click** on **Commands**. The Commands menu will appear.

2. **Click** on **Find File**. The Find File dialog box will open.

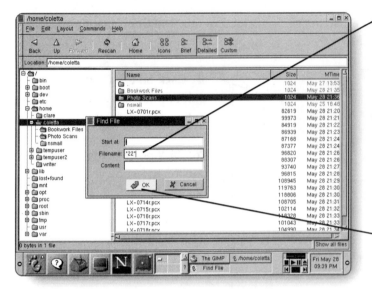

3. Click in the **Filename: text box** and **type** the **name** of the file.

NOTE

If you only know part of the file name, type that portion and include a wildcard character.

4. Click on **OK**. The Find file dialog box will open and show all directories in which the file can be found.

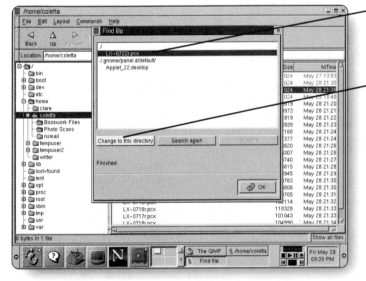

5. Click on the **directory** that contains the file you want. The directory will be selected.

6. Click on the **Change to this directory button**. The selected directory will be open in the file manager window.

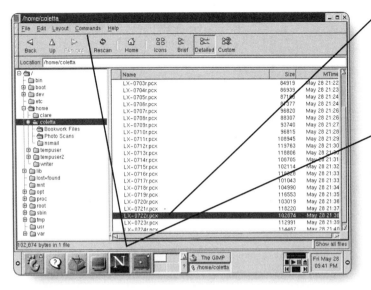

You'll see the file for which you were searching in the directory view.

NOTE

If this is not the file for which you were looking, open the Commands menu and select Find File. The Find File dialog box will contain the last search criteria you entered.

Working with Files on Your Desktop

If there's a file that you use frequently and you want to have it at your fingertips, move it onto your desktop.

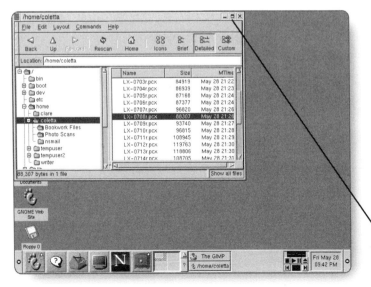

Moving the File to the Desktop

NOTE

You can also move entire directories onto the desktop using this same drag and drop method.

1. Resize the **file manager** so that the desktop area can be seen behind the window. The file manager window will be resized.

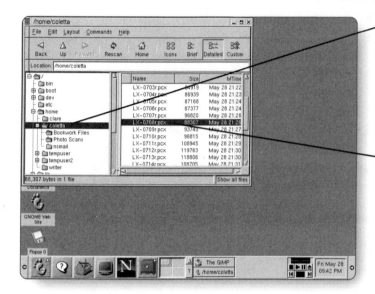

2. Open the **directory** that contains the file that you want to place on your desktop. The list of files contained in the directory will appear in the directory view.

3. Click and **hold** the **mouse pointer** on the file. The file will be selected.

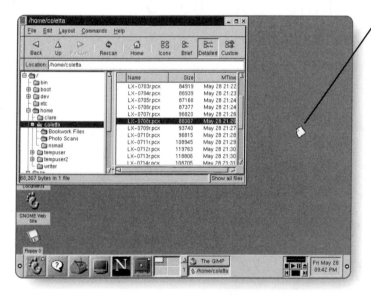

4. Drag the **file** to an empty area on the desktop.

5. Release the **mouse button**. An icon for the file will appear on your desktop.

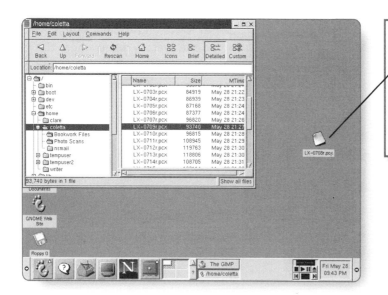

TIP

To move the icon to a different place on your desktop, click and drag the icon to the new position.

Opening the File

It is not always necessary to open the Linux application before you can open a file. Open the file and select the application in which you want to work. For example, you may have a picture that you started in a simple computer drawing program (such as XPaint) and now you want to edit the picture in a more sophisticated image-editing program (like The GIMP).

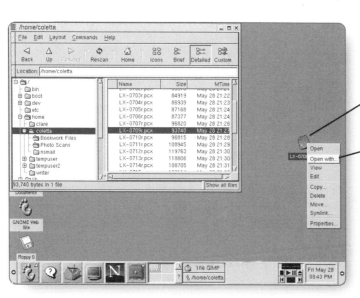

1. Right-click on a **file** to open. A menu will appear.

2. Click on **Open with**. The gmc dialog box will open.

TIP

You can also open files from the file manager window using this method.

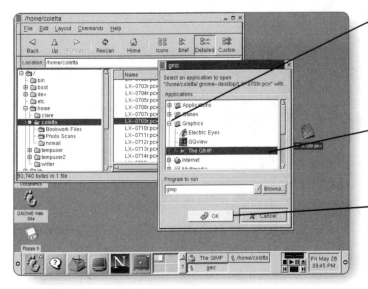

3. Click on the **plus sign** next to the system menu where the application is located. A list of the programs contained in that menu will appear.

4. Click on the **application** that you want to use. The application will be selected.

5. Click on **OK**. You'll see the file in the application window.

NOTE

The first time you use The GIMP, you will be asked to install some files so that the program can operate correctly. The program does all the work; you just need to confirm the installation by clicking on a couple of buttons.

8

Managing in a Multi-User Environment

Linux makes it easy for you to share one computer among several people. Each person is assigned an account and a password. Then, when each individual logs into Linux, the user will have a desktop and file system to customize. Each person's changes won't affect other users on the computer. Even though each user has a private area within Linux, all users can share files with each other. In this chapter, you'll learn how to:

- Create and edit user accounts
- Change your account password
- Form groups for file sharing
- Set file permissions for file sharing

Working with User Accounts

The first time you started Linux, you created a user account for yourself. You were shown a simple command that would set up the account. You can also set up accounts so that each user on the system can share files and directories with other users. Before you begin working with user accounts, you must be logged in as the superuser or root.

NOTE

If you need a refresher on logging into the root account, see Chapter 1.

Creating a New User Account

Each person using the Linux computer should have an account and password.

1. Click on the **Main Menu Button**. The Main Menu will appear.

2. Move the **mouse pointer** to System. The System menu will appear.

3. Click on **LinuxConf**. The gnome-linuxconf window will appear.

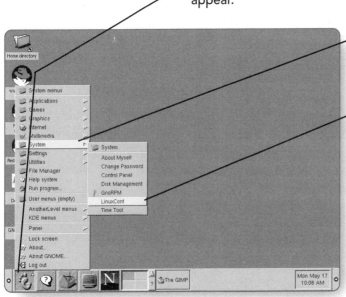

4. Scroll down the **Config list** in the left pane until you see the User accounts category. The list of configuration options for user accounts will be displayed.

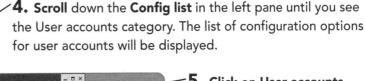

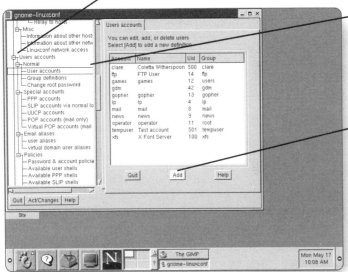

5. Click on **User accounts** under the Normal options. The right pane will appear showing all of the user accounts that are currently set up on the system.

6. Click on the **Add button** in the User accounts pane. The User account creation pane will appear.

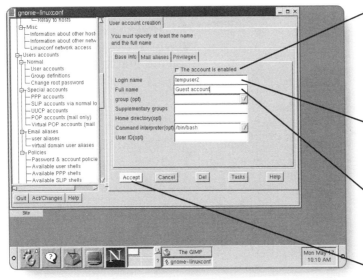

7. Click on the **check button** if The account is enabled check button is not selected (it should be recessed). The check button will be selected.

8. Click in the **Login name text box** and **type** a **user name** for the person.

9. Click in the **Full name text box** and **type** the person's **first and last names**.

10. Click on the **Accept button**. The Changing password pane will appear.

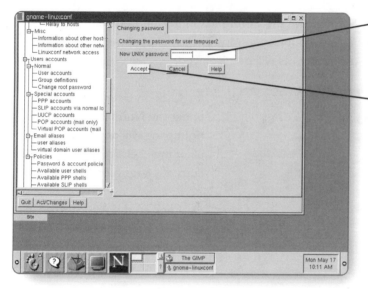

11. **Type** a **password** for the user account in the New Unix password: text box.

12. **Click** on the **Accept button**. The Changing password pane will change.

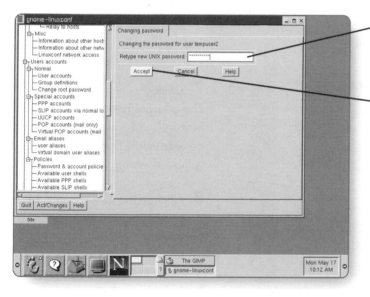

13. **Retype** the same **password** in the Retype new UNIX password: text box.

14. **Click** on the **Accept button**. The new user will be added to the list of user accounts.

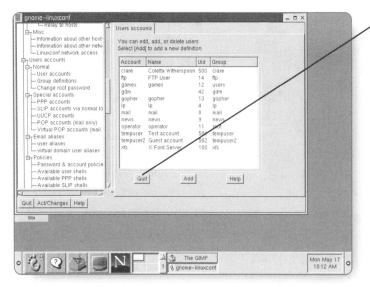

15. Click on the **Quit button**. The changes will be made to the system.

16. Click on the **Kill button**. The gnome-linuxconf window will close.

> **NOTE**
>
> If you see another screen titled "Status of System," click on the Activate the changes button to update the system.

Editing a User Account

Sometimes you'll need to change someone's name or password. Here's how you can change any needed details about the user.

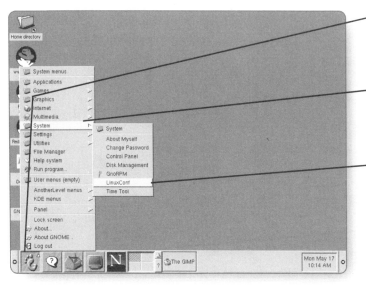

1. Click on the **Main Menu Button**. The Main Menu will appear.

2. Move the **mouse pointer** to System. The System menu will appear.

3. Click on **LinuxConf**. The gnome-linuxconf window will open.

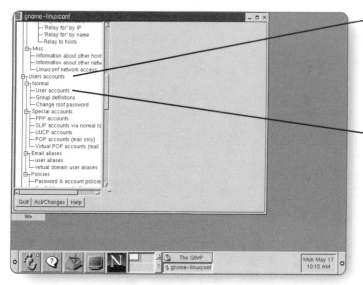

4. Scroll down the **Config list** in the left pane until you see the User accounts category. The list of configuration options for user accounts will be displayed.

5. Click on **User accounts** under the Normal options. The right pane will appear showing all the user accounts currently set up on the system.

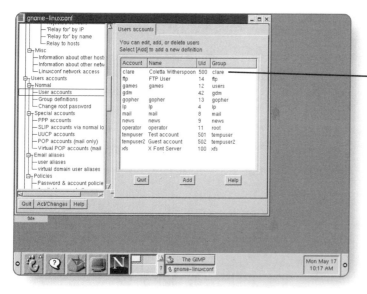

Changing User Information

1. Click on the **user account** in the Users accounts pane to which you want to make changes. The User information pane will appear and you can make a variety of changes.

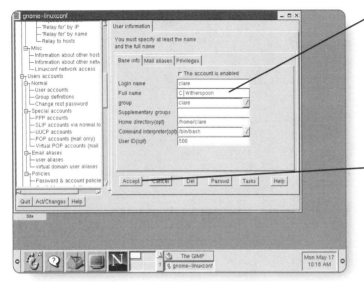

2. Click in the **Full name text box** and **type** the **first and last name** for the user. If you set up a user account using the method in Chapter 1, "Discovering Linux," this field will be blank.

3. Click on **Accept**. You'll be returned to the Users accounts tabs and see the changes in the list of user accounts.

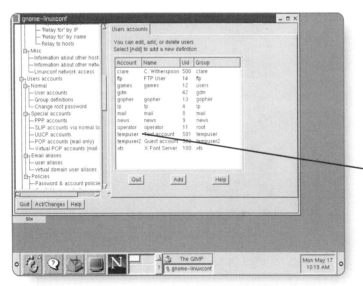

Changing the Password

If a number of people are using the same computer, it's a good idea to have everyone change passwords on a regular basis.

1. Click on the **user account** in the Users accounts pane for which you want to change the password. The User information pane will appear.

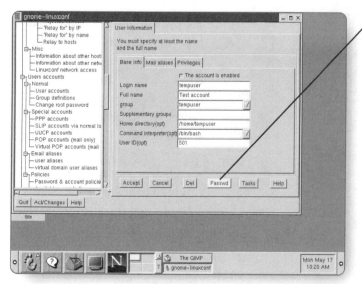

2. **Click** on the **Passwd button**. The Changing password pane will appear.

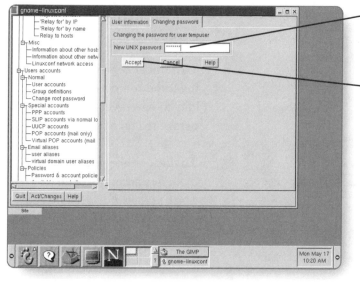

3. **Type** a different **password** in the New UNIX password: text box.

4. **Click** on the **Accept button**. A confirmation pane will appear.

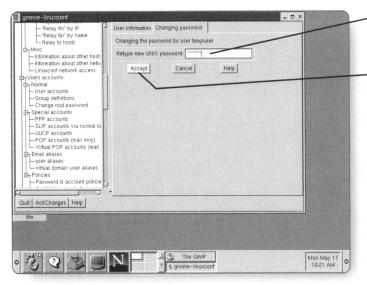

5. Type the same **password** that you typed in step 3.

6. Click on the **Accept button**. You will return to the list of user accounts.

Disabling a User's Account

If you need to restrict a user's access, you can easily keep the user's account in place but deny that person access to the system.

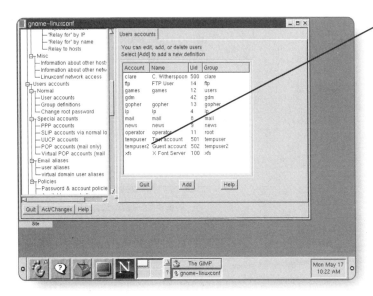

1. Click on the **user account** in the Users accounts pane that you want to disable. The User information pane will appear.

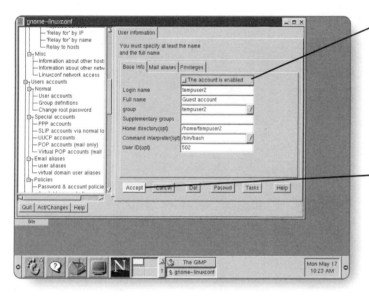

2. Click on the **The account is enabled check button**. The option will be deselected and any person trying to log in with this login name and password will not be given access to the system.

3. Click on **Accept**. You will return to the user list.

NOTE

When you want to enable this account, come back to this screen and click on the The account is enabled check button.

Deleting a User Account

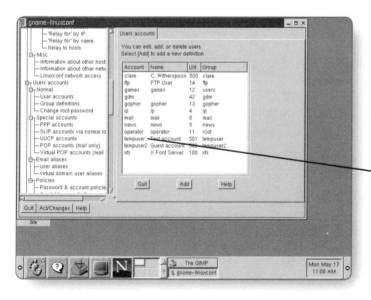

When a person will no longer be using the Linux computer, you can delete the account. If other users will need the files created by the deleted user, these files can be saved and used by others.

1. In the Users accounts pane, **click** on the **user account** that you want to remove. The User information pane will appear.

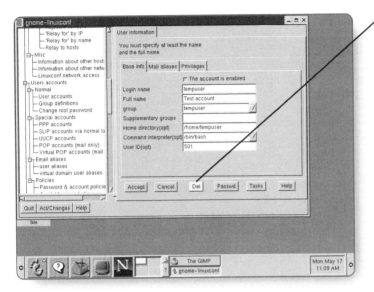

2. **Click** on the **Del button**. The Deleting account pane will appear.

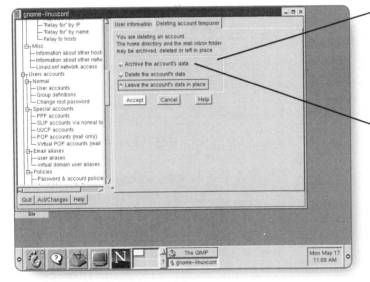

3. **Click** on an **option button** to specify how the files contained in the user's home directory will be handled. The option will be selected.

• **Archive the account's data**. This option compresses the files contained in the user's home directory into a single file. This file is placed in the /home directory, along with the directories for all of your user accounts, in a directory named /oldaccounts.

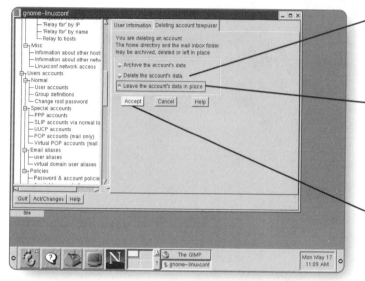

- **Delete the account's data.** This option removes the entire contents of the user's home directory.

- **Leave the account's data in place.** This option removes the user from the user list but leaves the user's home directory and contents in place.

4. **Click** on the **Accept button**. You will return to the user list and the user account will no longer appear in the list.

Allowing Users to Change Their Passwords

Individual users can change the password needed to access their user account from the GNOME interface. Before you do this for your own user account, log out of the root account and log back in as a user.

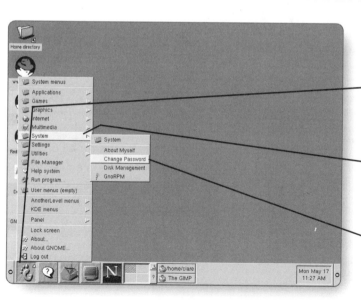

1. **Click** on the **Main Menu Button**. The Main Menu will appear.

2. **Move** the **mouse pointer** to System. The System menu will appear.

3. **Click** on **Change Password**. The Input dialog box will open.

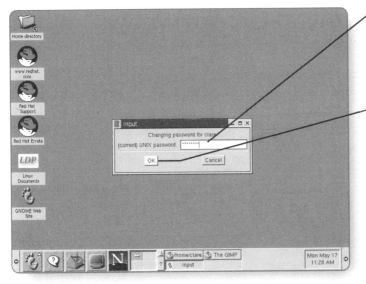

4. **Type** the **current password** used by the account in the (current) UNIX password: text box.

5. **Click** on **OK**. Another Input dialog box will appear.

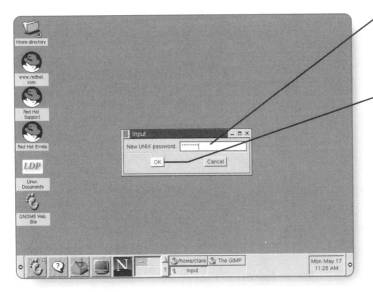

6. **Type** the **new password** that the user wants to use in the New UNIX password: text box.

7. **Click** on **OK**. The password for the user account will be changed.

Forming Groups

Groups allow you to share files between users. When users belong to the same group, they can share files created by the members of the group. The person who created the file can specify the type of access available to other members of the group.

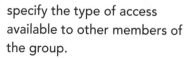

1. **Click** on the **Main Menu Button**. The Main Menu will appear.

2. **Move** the **mouse pointer** to System. The System menu will appear.

3. **Click** on **LinuxConf**. The GNOME-linuxconf window will open.

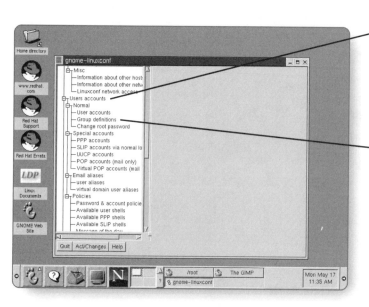

4. **Scroll down** the **Config list** in the left pane until you see the Users accounts category. The list of configuration options for user accounts will be displayed.

5. **Click** on **Group definitions** under the Normal options. The right pane will appear showing all the user groups currently set up on the system.

Creating a Group

To create file access between users on the Linux system, the first step is to form a group. Not every user on the system needs to belong to a group—only those people who need to share files (such as a workgroup). Some users may belong to several groups.

1. Click on the **Add button**. The Group specification pane will appear.

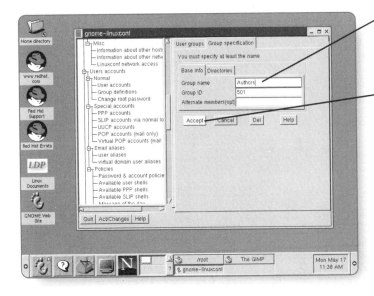

2. Click in the **Group name text box** and **type** a **name** for the group.

3. Click on the **Accept button**. You'll return to the list of user groups.

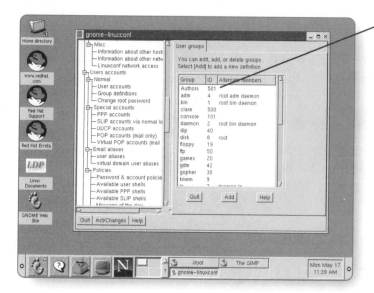

The group you just created will be added to the list.

NOTE

To make changes to the group, click on the group in the User groups pane. From here you can delete a group and create a default directory for the group to use to store files.

Assigning Users to a Group

Now that you've created a few groups, it's time to assign members to the group. Those people who have a reason to share files with each other should be placed in a separate group.

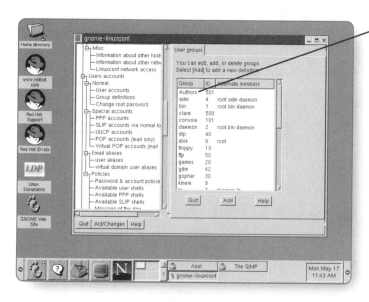

1. Click on the **group** to which you want to assign users. The Group specification pane for the selected group will appear.

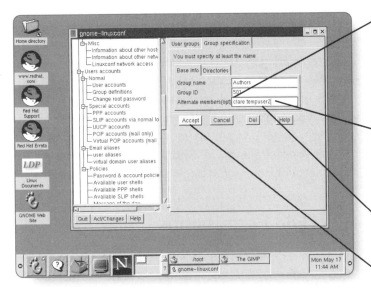

2. Click in the **Alternate members(opt) text box** and **type** the **user name** for the first person that you want to add to the group.

3. Press the **Spacebar** and **type** the **user name** for the second person that you want to add to the group.

4. Add more **user names** as needed.

5. Click on the **Accept button**. The User groups pane will appear.

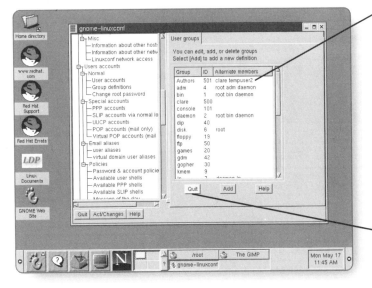

You'll see the user names listed in the Alternate members column.

TIP

You can assign a group to a user when you are editing the user's account.

6. Click on the **Quit button** when you are finished.

Sharing Files with a Group

Multi-user operating systems like Linux have different ways of handling file management than single-user systems like DOS. Sometimes you'll want to share files with other users. At the same time, you might not want to share everything with everyone so you need to set up your files to discriminate about what you share and with whom. You'll want to be in your user account before you begin setting file permissions.

Setting File Permissions

The assignment of file permissions to control user access works on a system of file access being permitted or denied. You can easily give read-only or write-access to yourself or to members of a group.

1. Double-Click on the **Home directory icon** on the desktop. The File manager will appear with your Home directory displayed.

2. Click on the **directory** that contains the file you want to share with others in your group. The directory contents will appear.

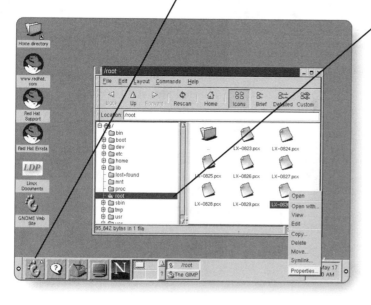

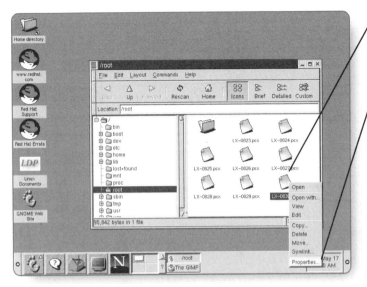

3. Right-click on the **file** that you want to share with others in a group. A menu will appear.

4. Click on **Properties**. The Properties dialog box for the selected file will appear.

TIP

You can set file permissions for several files at once. Select all the files that will need the same file permissions.

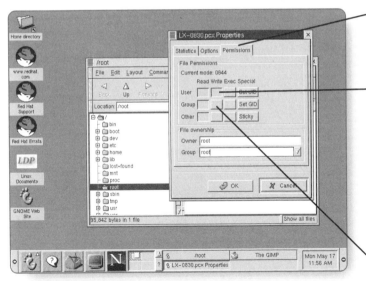

5. Click on the **Permissions tab**. The File Permissions tab will come to the top of the stack.

6. Click on the **Write check button** in the User area if the owner of the file does not want to be able to make any changes to the file. The check button will be deselected and the owner of the file will have read-only access.

7. Click on the **Write check button** in the Group area if the owner of the file wants other members of the group to be able to make changes to the file. The check button will be selected.

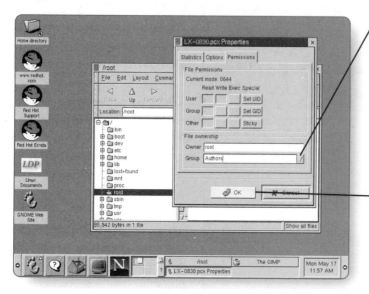

8. Click on the **down arrow** next to the Group list box. A drop-down list will appear.

9. Click on the **group** that needs to have access to the file. The selected group will appear in the list box.

10. Click on **OK** if you are satisfied with your choices. The dialog box will close and the file permissions will be set.

9

Maintaining Linux

The only time you'll want to log into Linux as the superuser is when you make changes to the entire Linux system, not just an individual user's account. There are a few things you can do to keep on top of your Linux system. One of the most important is having boot and recovery disks on hand. These two disks will help immensely when you run into a problem. In this chapter, you'll learn how to:

- Find information about your computer system
- Mount floppy drives to be used by Linux
- Create a recovery disk set
- Check for available disk space
- Change the time on your computer clock

Finding System Information

If you need to find out some information about the system running your computer, there's an easy way to do it. You can find out which Linux distribution you're running along with the operating system version and kernel. You don't need to be in the superuser account to find this information because you can find it if you are logged into a user account.

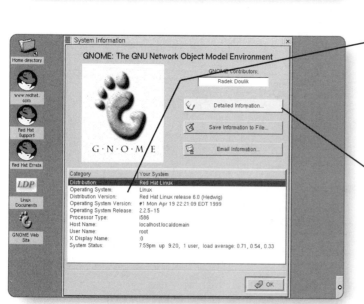

1. Click on the **Main Menu Button**. The Main Menu will appear.

2. Move the **mouse pointer** to Utilities. The Utilities menu will appear.

3. Click on **System Info**. The System Information window will open.

At the bottom of the window, you'll see the Linux distribution name and version, the kernel number, and some information about your computer and its current usage.

4. Click on the **Detailed Information button**. The Detail System Information dialog box will open and the Disk Information tab will be at the top of the stack.

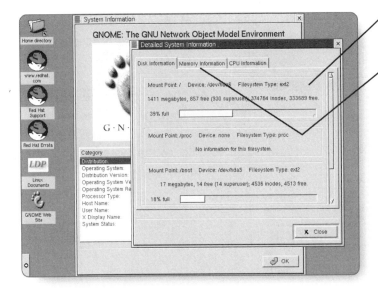

Note the total hard drive space and the amount of free space.

5. Click on the **Memory Information tab**. The memory Information tab will come to the top of the stack.

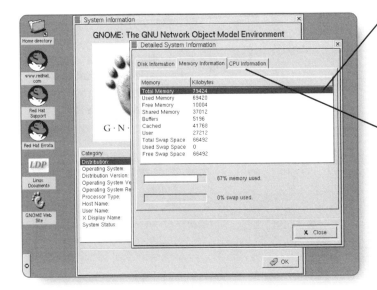

The Total Memory is the amount of RAM installed on your system. You'll also notice how much memory is currently being used.

6. Click on the **CPU Information tab**. The CPU Information tab will come to the top of the stack.

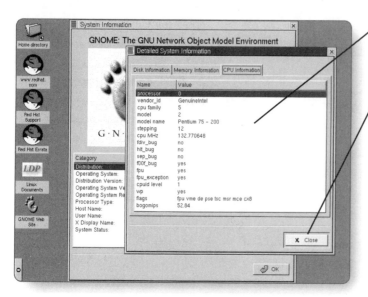

All of the information relating to your computer's processor chip is located in this dialog box.

7. Click on the **Close button.** The Detail System Information dialog box will close and you'll return to the System Information window.

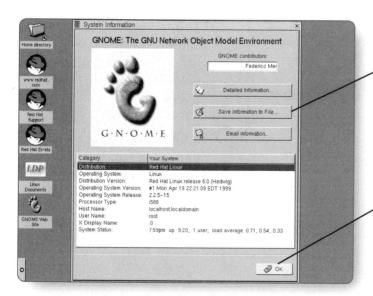

TIP

If you want to print the information, click on the Save Information to File button. You can save the information as a text file and print it later.

8. Click on **OK**. The System Information window will close.

Mounting a Floppy Disk Drive

Before you can copy files from the Linux file system to a floppy disk, you'll need to mount your computer's floppy disk drive. By mounting the drive, you are telling Linux where the drive resides and what type of file system it uses. You have a choice of two types of file systems. You can either use Linux-formatted disks to use on other Linux machines, or you can create a DOS file system so that you can transfer files between a Linux computer and a DOS or Windows computer. You must be logged in as superuser or root to mount a drive.

Creating a Linux Floppy Drive.

1. Click on the **Main Menu Button**. The Main Menu will appear.

2. Move the **mouse pointer** to System. The System menu will appear.

3. Click on **LinuxConf**. The gnome-linuxconf window will open.

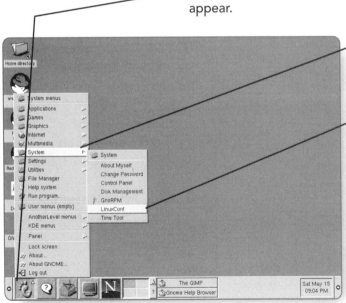

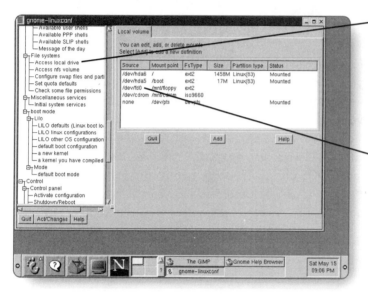

4. Scroll down to the **File systems category** and **click** on the **Access local drive option**. The Local volume pane will appear to the right of the window.

5. Click on **/dev/fd0**. The Volume specification pane will appear.

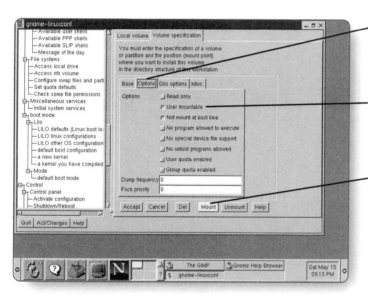

6. Click on the **Options tab**. The Options tab will come to the top of the stack.

7. Click on the **User mountable option button**. The option will be selected.

8. Click on the **Mount button**. The Mount file system pane will appear.

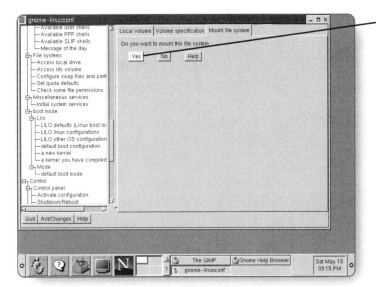

9. Click on the **Yes button**. The Please note pane will appear.

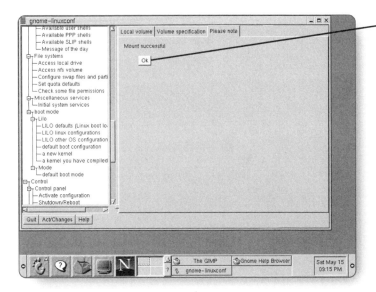

10. Click on the **OK button**. You will return to the Volume specification pane.

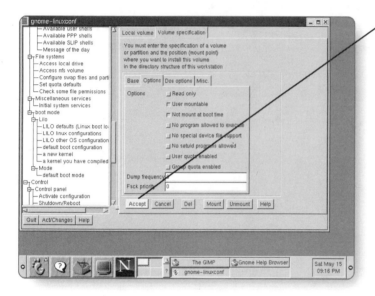

11. **Click** on the **Accept button**. You will return to the Local volume pane.

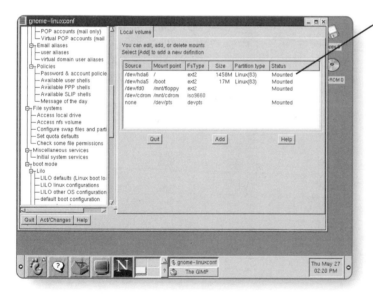

You'll see that the floppy drive has been mounted in the Status column.

Creating a DOS Floppy Drive

If you want to copy files onto a floppy disk and use that disk on a computer that uses DOS or Windows, you'll want to set the file system for the floppy drive to operate in MS-DOS Format.

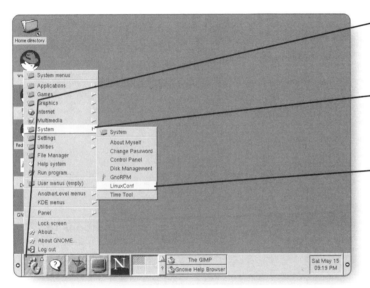

1. **Click** on the **Main Menu Button**. The Main Menu will appear.

2. **Move** the **mouse pointer** to System. The System menu will appear.

3. **Click** on **LinuxConf**. The gnome-linuxconf window will open.

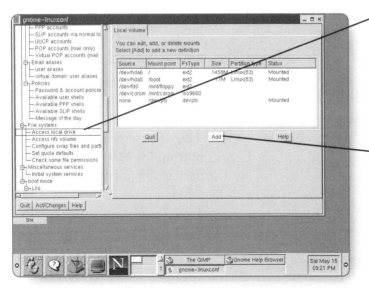

4. **Scroll down** to the **File systems category** and **click** on the **Access local drive option**. The Local volume pane will appear to the right of the window.

5. **Click** on the **Add button**. The Volume specification pane will appear.

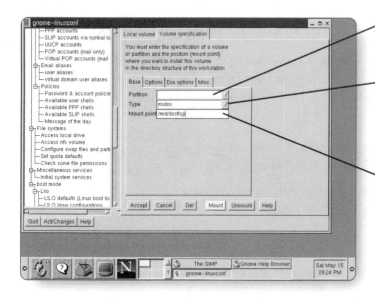

6. **Click** in the **Partition text box** and **type /dev/fd0**.

7. **Click** on the **down arrow** next to the Type list box and **click** on **msdos**. The selected type will appear in the list box.

8. **Click** in the **Mount point text box** and **type /mnt/dosflop**.

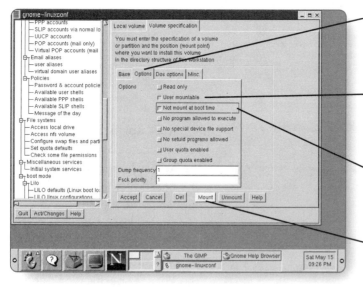

9. **Click** on the **Options tab**. The Options tab will come to the top of the stack.

10. **Click** on the **User mountable option button**. The option will be selected.

11. **Click** on the **Not mount at boot time option button**. The option will be selected.

12. **Click** on the **Mount button**. The Mount file system pane will appear.

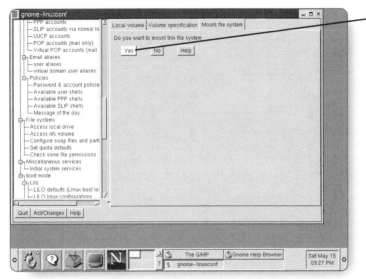

13. Click on the **Yes button**. The Please note pane will appear.

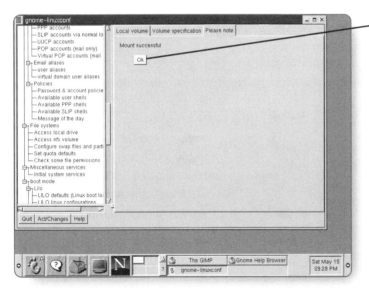

14. Click on the **OK button**. You will return to the Volume specification pane.

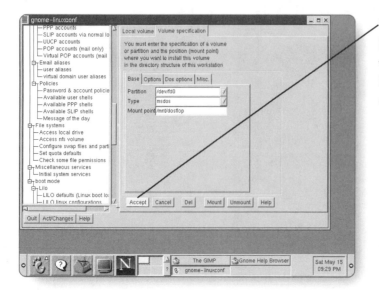

15. **Click** on the **Accept button**. The gnome-linuxconf window will close and you will have access to the floppy disk drive.

Mounting the Floppy Drive in the User Account

The floppy drive needs to be mounted before a user can have access to the floppy drive from their account.

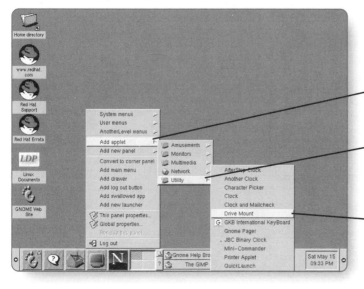

1. **Right-click** on an **empty area** on the GNOME Panel. A menu will appear.

2. **Move** the **mouse pointer** to Add applet. A menu will appear.

3. **Move** the **mouse pointer** to Utility. Another menu will appear.

4. **Click** on **Drive Mount**. A floppy drive icon will be added to the GNOME Panel.

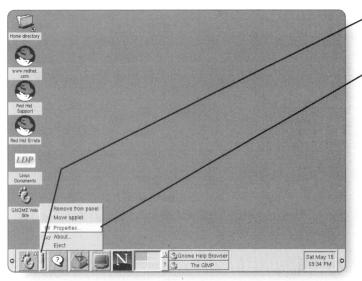

5. Right-click on the **floppy drive icon**. A menu will appear.

6. Click on **Properties**. The Drive Mount Settings dialog box will open.

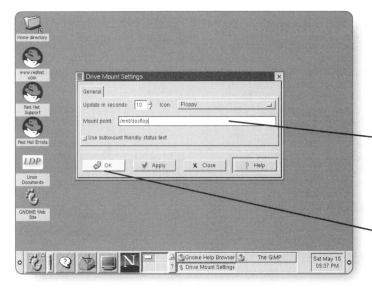

7a. If you want to mount the Linux floppy drive, **click** in the **Mount point text box** and **type /mnt/floppy**.

OR

7b. If you want to mount the MS-DOS floppy drive, **click** in the **Mount point text box** and type **/mnt/dosflop**.

8. Click on **OK**. The Drive Mount Settings dialog box will close and if you hold the mouse pointer over the floppy icon on the GNOME panel, you'll see a tooltip that says that the floppy drive is mounted.

Preparing a Recovery Disk Set

In the hopefully unlikely case that your Linux fails you, you'll need a boot disk and a recovery disk to help alleviate your troubles.

Creating a Boot Disk

When you installed Linux, you were given the opportunity to create a boot disk. If you didn't create one at that time, you can still give yourself some peace of mind by creating a boot disk now.

1. **Place** a **floppy disk** in your computer's floppy disk drive. You'll want to label this disk "Boot Image Disk."

2. **Click** on the **GNOME Terminal icon** on the GNOME Panel. The Terminal window will open on your screen.

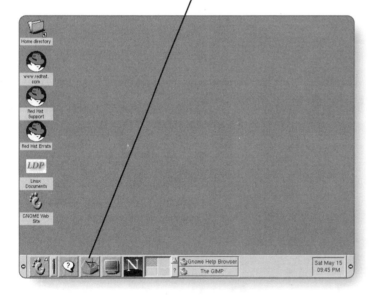

3. Type **cd /lib/modules** and **press Enter**. The directory will be changed to the modules directory in which the files needed for the boot disk are located.

4. Type **ls** and **press Enter**. The kernel version number for your Linux operating system will be displayed and you will know which kernel to copy to the boot disk.

5. Type **mkbootdisk—device /dev/fd0 2.2.5-15** and **press Enter**. A confirmation prompt will appear.

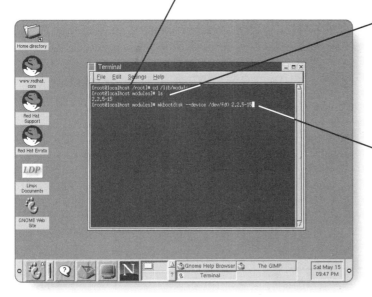

6. Press Enter. The boot information will be copied to the disk. When the process is complete, you'll return to the command prompt.

7. Type **cd** and **press Enter**. You will return to the root prompt.

8. Click on the **Kill button**. The Terminal window will close.

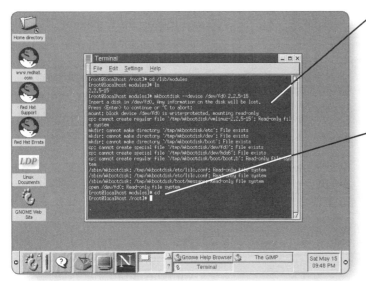

Creating a Recovery Disk

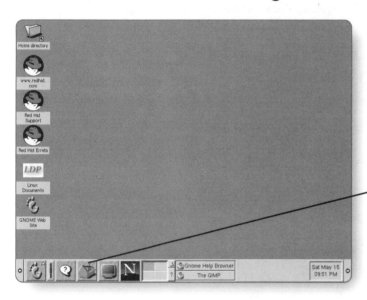

The recovery disk will help you perform system diagnostics to determine why your Linux is not operating as expected.

1. Place the first **Red Hat Linux CD** in your computer's CD-ROM drive.

2. Click on **GNOME Terminal**. The Terminal window will open on your screen.

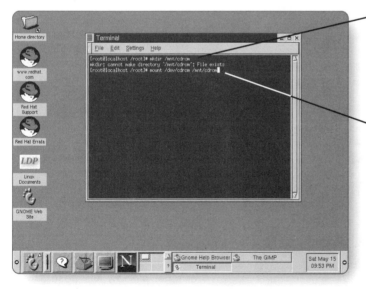

3. Type mkdir /mnt/cdrom and **press Enter**. The directory will be created. If you get a message saying that the file already exists, everything is still OK.

4. Type mount /dev/cdrom /mnt/cdrom and **press Enter**. You'll see a message saying that the CD is write-protected.

NOTE

If your Linux system does not recognize /dev/cdrom, you'll need to replace /dev/cdrom in the command with the appropriate device name for your CD-ROM.

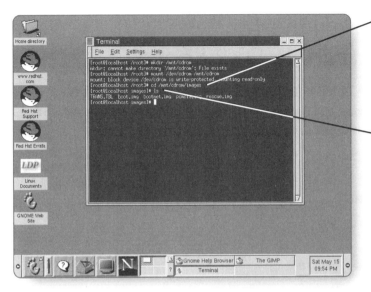

5. Type cd /mnt/cdrom/images and **press Enter**. The current directory will be changed to the images subdirectory on the CD-ROM.

6. Type ls and **press Enter**. The list of files contained in the directory will appear. You are looking for the file named "rescue.img."

7. Put a **disk** in your floppy disk drive. Label this disk "Rescue Disk."

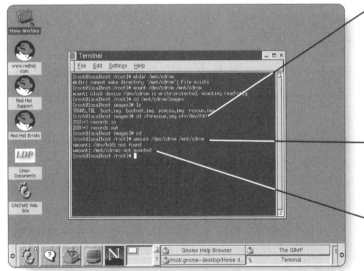

8. Type dd if=rescue.img of=/dev/fd0 and **press Enter**. The file will be copied to the disk. When the copy process is complete, you will return to the command prompt.

9. Type cd and **press Enter**. You will return to the root prompt.

10. Type umount /dev/cdrom /mnt/cdrom and **press Enter**. You will now be able to take the CD out of the CD-ROM drive.

11. Click on the **Kill button**. The Terminal window will close.

Checking for Available Disk Space

The GNOME DiskFree is a small utility that shows you how much free space is available on the different partitions and hard drives on your computer system.

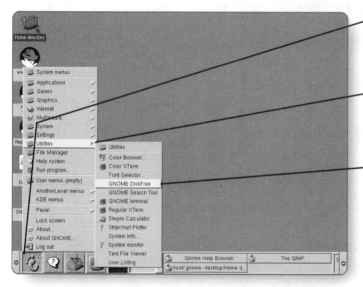

1. **Click** on the **Main Menu Button**. The Main Menu will appear.

2. **Move** the **mouse pointer** to Utilities. The Utilities menu will appear.

3. **Click** on **GNOME DiskFree**. The DiskFree utility will open.

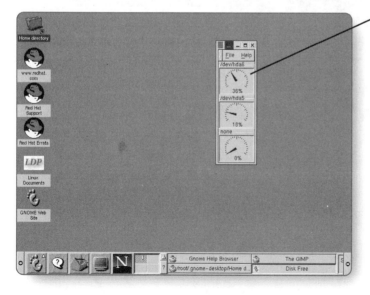

Notice the different dials for each partition and hard drive. The dials show you the amount of free space available.

Resetting the Clock

You may find that the clock on the GNOME Panel is off by a few minutes. Here's what you can do to keep the exact time.

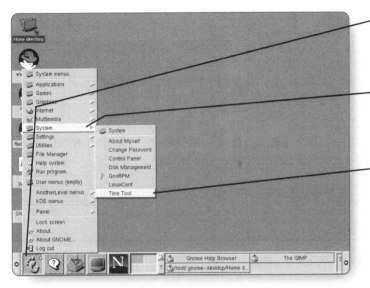

1. **Click** on the **Main Menu Button**. The Main Menu will appear.

2. **Move** the **mouse pointer** to System. The System menu will appear.

3. **Click** on **Time Tool**. The Time Machine will open.

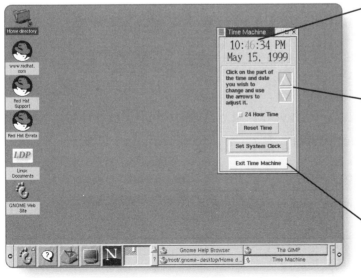

4. **Click** on the **hour, minute,** or **date** that you want to change. The hour, minute, or date will be selected.

5. **Click** the **up** and **down arrows** until the time you want is displayed.

6. **Change** any other time or date **elements**.

7. **Click** on the **Exit Time Machine button**. The Time Machine will close and your system clock will be updated to show the change.

Part II Review Questions

1. Where are your user files located in the Linux file system? *See "Opening the File System" in Chapter 6*

2. What are the three different ways in which you can view the contents of a directory? *See "Browsing the File System" in Chapter 6*

3. In which directory on the Linux file system will you be storing most of the files you create? *See "Creating Directories" in Chapter 7*

4. How do you make a copy of a file and move it to another directory? *See "Copying and Moving Files" in Chapter 7*

5. Which Linux utility allows you to create and edit user accounts? *See "Working with User Accounts" in Chapter 8*

6. Can users on the Linux system change their own passwords? *See "Allowing Users to Change Their Password" in Chapter 8*

7. How do you add users to a group so that they can share files? *See "Forming Groups" in Chapter 8*

8. What kinds of information can you find out about your computer and Linux system? *See "Finding System Information" in Chapter 9*

9. Name the two types of file systems that can be used to mount floppy disks. *See "Mounting a Floppy Disk Drive" in Chapter 9*

10. Why is it important to create a recovery disk set? *See "Preparing a Recovery Disk Set" in Chapter 9*

PART III

Making Linux Work for You

10

Working with Files

Now that you've had some fun playing with the Linux operating system and the GNOME user interface, it's time to try your hand at some of the applications that were installed with your Linux. All software applications allow you to create a new file and to save that file on your computer's hard drive. In previous chapters, you learned about the Linux file system and how to move around within the file system. Now it's time to use an application to see how the Linux applications interact with the file system. In this chapter, you'll learn how to:

- Open gnotepad+ and create a new file
- Perform basic text selection and editing commands
- Save a file
- Close and reopen a file

Creating a New File

You first need to open a Linux application and create a new file. Some applications will open with a blank page, whereas other applications make you create your own blank page. You'll learn how to use gnotepad+ to perform basic file tasks in Linux.

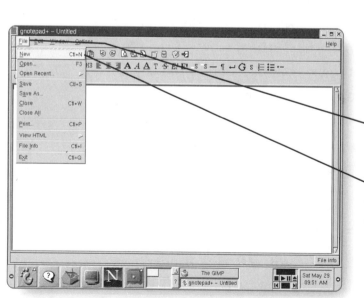

1. Click on the **Main Menu Button**. The main menu will appear.

2. Move the **mouse pointer** to Applications. The Applications menu will appear.

3. Click on **gnotepad+**. The gnotepad application will open and a blank page will appear ready for you to start typing.

Some Linux applications do not display a blank page. If this is the case, you'll need to open a new document.

4. Click on **File**. The File menu will appear.

5. Click on **New**. A blank page will appear in the application window.

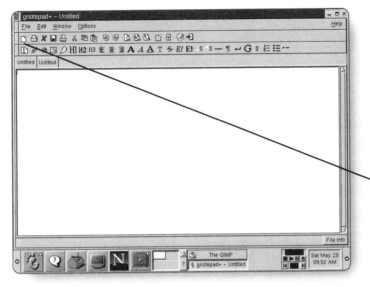

Some applications display a toolbar that contains buttons for a number of frequently-used commands. Hold the mouse pointer over a toolbar button to display a tooltip that explains the command a button executes.

6. Click on the **New File button**. A blank page will appear in the application window.

Working with Text

When you open a blank page, notice a vertical bar in the upper-left corner of the page. This is the insertion point, and it is where text will appear as you type. To follow the instructions that follow, type a few paragraphs into the gnotepad window.

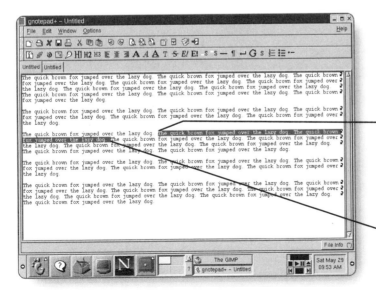

Selecting Text

Before you can begin editing text in most applications, you need to know how to select text.

1. Click and **hold** the **mouse pointer** at the place where you want to begin the selection. The insertion bar will appear in the selected position.

2. Drag the **mouse** to the **end** of the selection. The selected text will be highlighted.

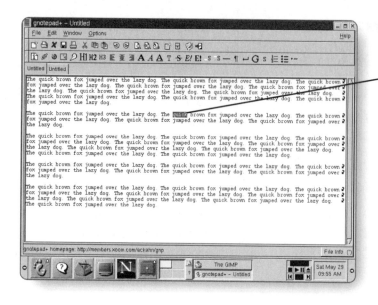

3. Try out these **shortcut methods** for selecting text.

- To select one word, click twice on the word.

- To select a paragraph, click three times on the paragraph.

Copying and Deleting Text

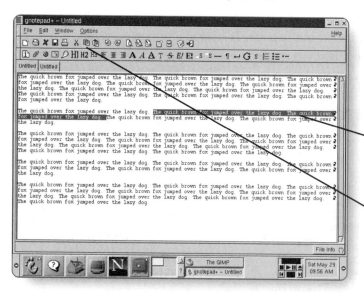

You'll use the copy and delete functions when you are rearranging text. You'll also get some practice using toolbar buttons.

1. Select the **text** that you want to copy. The text will be selected.

2. Click on the **Copy Text button**. The text will be copied to the Clipboard.

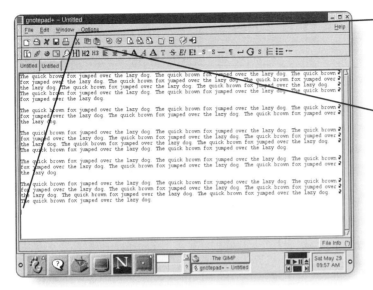

3. Click on the **place** where you want to place a copy of the text. The insertion bar will appear in the selected position.

4. Click on the **Paste Text button**. The text will be copied to the new position.

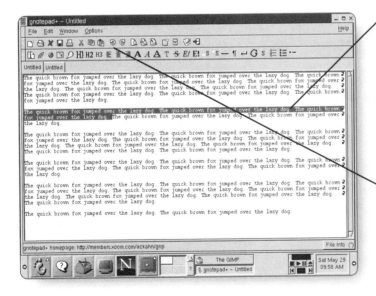

5. Select the **text** that you want to delete. The text will be selected.

6. Press the **Delete key**. The text will be deleted.

TIP

If you made a mistake and want to reverse the last action you performed, click on the Undo button. You can undo more than one action.

Saving a File

The importance of saving your work cannot be emphasized enough. Anyone who uses a computer has lost valuable work at one time or another. Save your work regularly; it only takes a few mouse clicks to save hours of work.

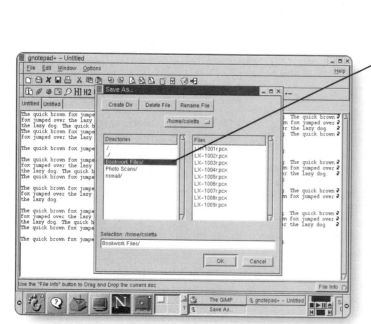

1. Click on the **Save File button**. The Save As dialog box will open.

TIP

If you want to have another copy of a document, open the File menu and select Save As. You can then save the document using a different file name.

---

2. Double-click on the **directory** in which you want to save the file from the Directories list. The directory will open to show the subdirectories in the Directories list and the files contained in the directory in the Files list.

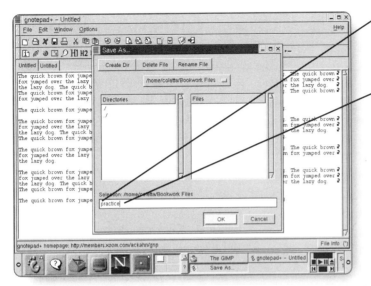

3. Click in the **Selection: text box.** The insertion point will be in the text box.

4. Type a **name** for the file. The name will appear in the text box.

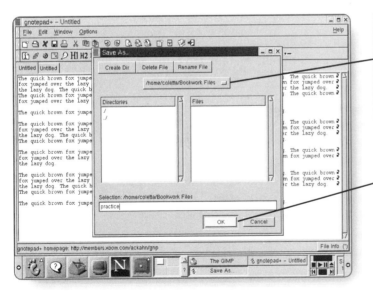

TIP

If you want to go back to a previous directory that you had open, click on the list box and select a directory from the list.

5. Click on **OK**. The file will be saved in the directory you specified.

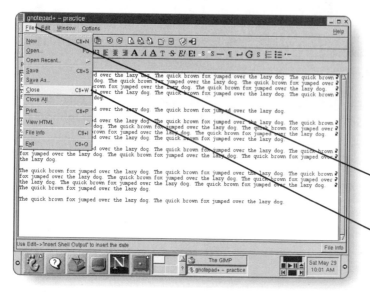

Closing a File

When you are finished working with a document, you can close the file. It's easy to close the file but still leave your application open.

1. Click on **File**. The File menu will appear.

2. Click on **Close**. The file will close and the gnotepad+ window will stay open.

Opening an Existing File

You can open any document that you've saved. You'll need to go back to the file system and remember where you put the file.

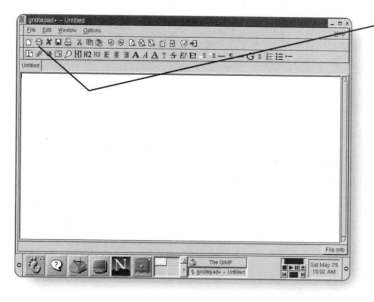

1. Click on the **Open File button**. The Open File dialog box will open.

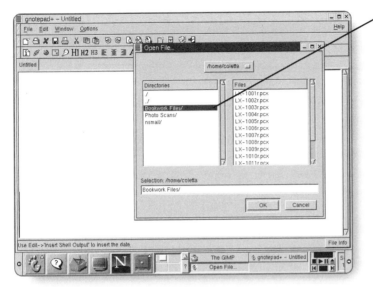

2. Double-click on the **directory** where the file is located. The list of files contained in that directory will appear.

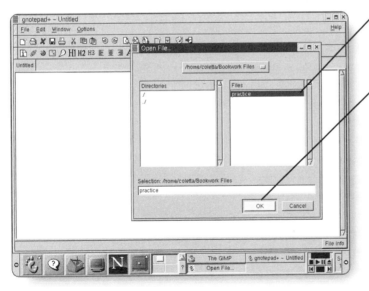

3. Click on the **file** that you want to open. The file will be selected.

4. Click on **OK**. The file will appear in the application window and you can resume working on the file.

11

Drawing with XPaint

XPaint is a color-image editing tool that comes with Linux. It has many features in common with other computer paint programs and also contains features found in some of the more complex graphics applications. Drawings created or edited in XPaint can be saved in many formats for use in other applications or operating systems. In this chapter, you'll learn how to:

- Start a new drawing in XPaint
- Draw basic shapes
- Add text to a picture
- Save a drawing to use later

Getting Started with XPaint

XPaint is a fun drawing program that is easy to learn, yet still contains some features found in sophisticated graphics programs. Take some time away from the technical side of your computer and draw some pictures to hang on your refrigerator.

Opening XPaint

1. Click on the **Main Menu Button**. The Main Menu will appear.

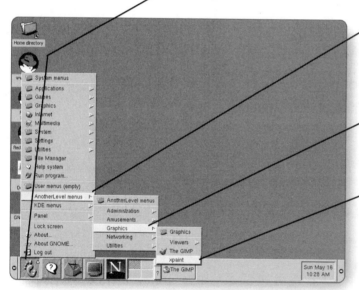

2. Move the **mouse pointer** to the AnotherLevel menus. The AnotherLevel menus listing will appear.

3. Move the **mouse pointer** to Graphics. The Graphics menu will appear.

4. Click on **xpaint**. The XPaint toolbox will appear.

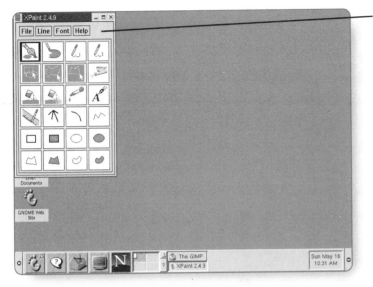

The XPaint toolbox is where you select the tools to create a variety of artistic works.

NOTE

You can move and resize the toolbox window using the methods in Chapter 2, "Working with Program Windows."

Getting Familiar with the XPaint Toolbox

The XPaint toolbox is the control center and repository of the drawing tools that are used in the Paint windows. It is here that you set options applicable to the paint window.

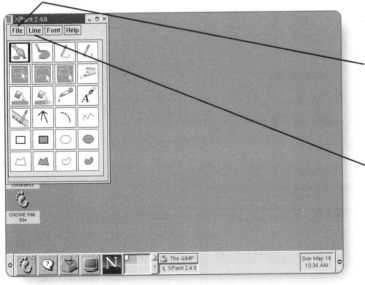

At the top of the XPaint Toolbox is a menu with four choices:

- **File menu**. This menu is where you create a workspace by loading an image file or creating an empty canvas.

- **Line menu**. The Line menu controls line width settings for any line that is drawn.

● **Font menu**. Use this menu to select the font to apply to text used in the drawing.

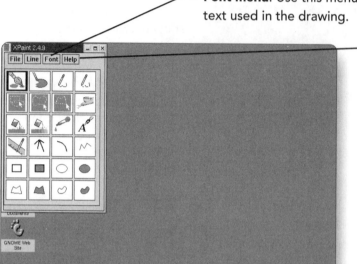

● **Help menu**. This choice opens the XPaint Help Browser. You'll find detailed information about the tools and features of the program in the Help menu. Some very useful information is provided in an interactive HTML format.

The rest of the toolbox contains buttons for a number of drawing objects and effects.

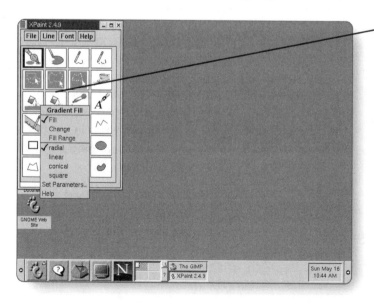

1. **Right-click** on a **toolbox button**. A menu will appear showing the name of the button at the top of the menu, followed by the commands that can be used to change the way the tool works.

Creating a New, Blank Canvas

It's time to open a workspace on your screen to begin your work of art.

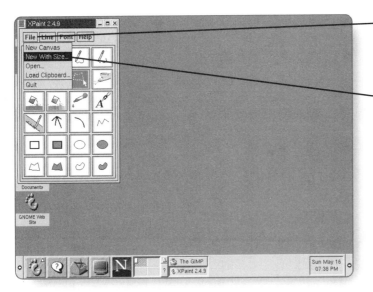

1. **Click** and **hold** on the **File menu**. The File menu will appear.

2. **Move** the **mouse pointer** to New With Size and **release** the **mouse button**. The Size select dialog box will open.

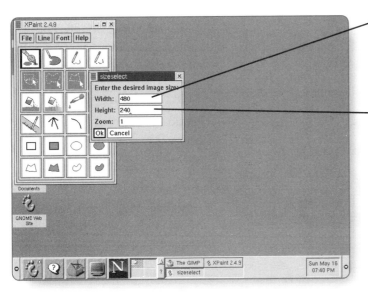

3. **Double-click** in the **Width: text box** and **type** the **number** of pixels wide you want the new picture.

4. **Double-click** in the **Height: text box** and **type** the **number** of pixels high you want the new picture.

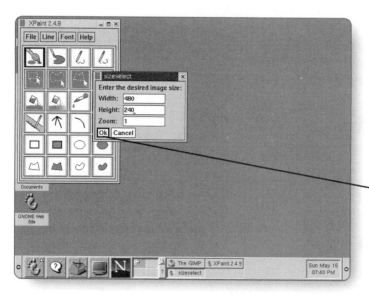

5. Click on **OK**. The paint window will appear with a blank canvas on which to begin your work.

Understanding the Paint Window

When you select New Canvas from the Toolbox File menu, XPaint opens a window on the desktop where your image or drawing will be displayed and where the tools from the toolbox will be used. You'll notice a number of different tools. Take a little time to explore the paint window.

Across the top of the Paint window is the menu bar that contains the commands you will use with XPaint.

- **File menu.** This menu contains commands to save the image file on the current Paint window.

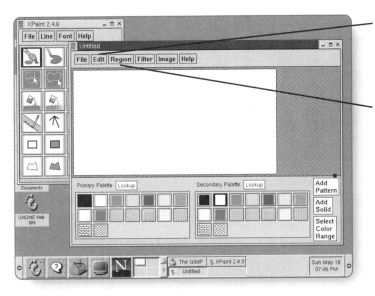

- **Edit menu.** The usual cut and paste, duplicate, and redo and undo choices are on this menu.

- **Region menu.** This menu applies some of the same operators as the Edit menu plus cropping abilities for a selected region, not the whole image.

- **Filter menu.** This menu contains image-processing operations that can be applied to the currently selected region.

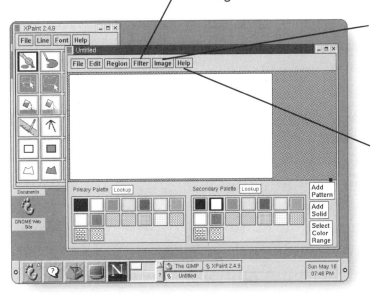

- **Image menu.** This menu allows you to create Snap and Grid lines that can be applied to the current image or the entire canvas to assist editing.

- **Help menu.** This menu opens the XPaint Help Browser for the Paint window section of the XPaint help system.

At the bottom of the Paint window are two palettes for selecting colors.

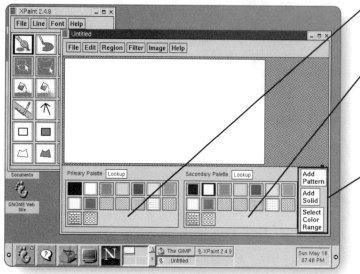

- **Primary Palette.** This palette sets the color for any lines that are drawn.

- **Secondary Palette.** You can set the color for the fill for any objects (such as squares and circles) drawn with this palette.

- **Add Pattern, Add Solid, and Select Color Range.** These three tiles allow you to add solid colors, patterns, or a range of colors to both the Primary Palette and Secondary Palette.

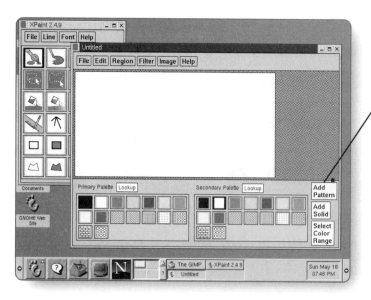

You may find that the few colors and patterns that are included on the color palettes won't work for the picture you have in mind.

- The Add Pattern tile brings up the Pattern Editor, which allows you to create your own patterns in a variety of colors.

TIP

Double-click on any color or pattern icons in the palettes to open the Color Selector or the Pattern Editor. You can make changes to the selected color or pattern from these two dialog boxes.

Creating Great Graphics with XPaint

The best way to get started with a graphics program is to play with its basic tools. Get comfortable creating boxes and circles and drawing lines with pencils and brushes. There's lots you can do with XPaint, so take your time and explore.

Drawing Shapes

Drawing with a mouse is a difficult skill to acquire, but with patience and persistence, you can achieve some great results. XPaint also has tools and Help tips to get you going.

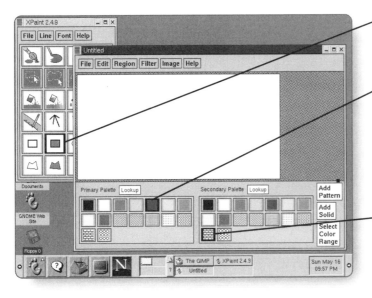

1. Click the **Filled Box tool** in the Toolbox. The tool will be selected.

2. Click on a **color or pattern** in the Primary Palette located at the bottom left of the Paint window. The line (outline) color for your drawing will be selected.

3. Click on a **color or pattern** in the Secondary palette. The fill color for your drawing will be selected.

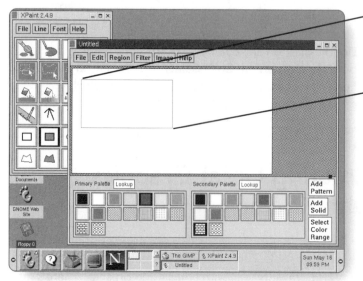

4. **Click and hold** the **mouse pointer** in the upper-left corner of the blank canvas.

5. **Drag** the **mouse pointer** down and to the right. An outline of the shape will appear.

6. **Release** the **mouse button** when the shape is the size you want. The shape will appear on the canvas and be filled with the color that you chose from the secondary palette.

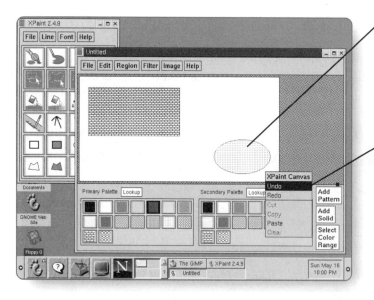

7. **Try** out a **different shape** and **choose different colors** from the two palettes.

TIP

If you want to remove a shape you just created, right-click on the canvas. Select Undo from the menu that appears.

Selecting and Moving a Shape

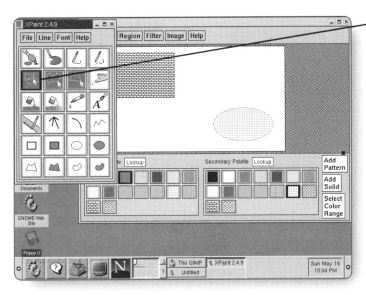

1. Right-click on the **Select Box/Ellipse tool**. A menu will appear.

2. Click on the **type of shape** you want to select. The type will be selected and the menu will close.

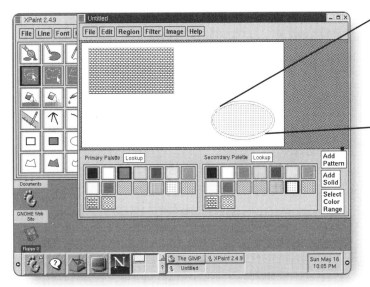

3. Click and hold at the **upper-left corner** of the shape and **drag** the **mouse pointer** to the lower-right corner. An outline will appear around the shape.

4. Release the **mouse button**. Selection handles will appear around the shape.

> ### TIP
> To resize a shape, click and drag the selection handles. Selection handles are the small square boxes that appear around the border of the shape.

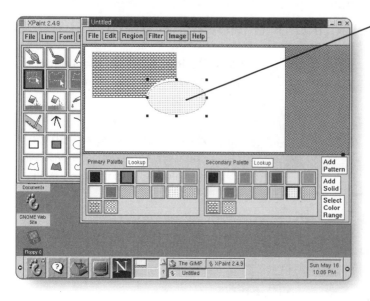

5. Place the **mouse pointer** over the shape you want to move. The mouse pointer will change to a four-pointed arrow.

6. Click and **hold** on the **shape** and **drag** it to a **new position**. The shape will move with the mouse pointer.

7. Release the **mouse button** when the shape is in the desired location.

Experimenting with Brush Strokes

If you want to draw a line, you can use a variety of brushes, pencils, lines, and sprays. Each one creates a different look. You can change the color, shape, and size of these tools to create the desired effect.

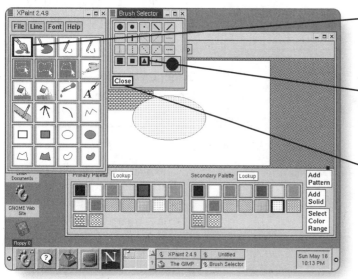

1. Double-click on the **Brush tool**. The Brush Selector dialog box will open.

2. Click on a **brush shape** in the Brush Selector. The brush shape will be selected.

3. Click on **Close**. The dialog box will close and the mouse pointer will change to the selected brush shape you selected.

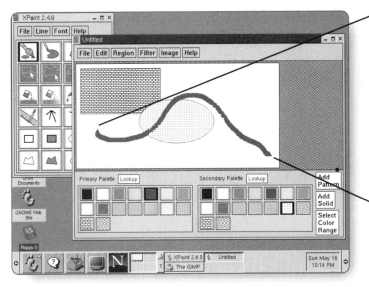

4. **Click** and **hold** on the **place** on the canvas where you want to start the brush stroke.

5. **Drag** the **mouse pointer** around the canvas to create the line. The line will appear in the path the mouse pointer followed.

6. **Release** the **mouse button** when you are finished drawing the line.

Adding Text to Your Picture

The Font Browser enables you to use any available font with the painting operation you are doing in the paint window. The Font Browser is actually pretty smart: it helps guide your choice of fonts by altering the list of variables to match your choices as you go.

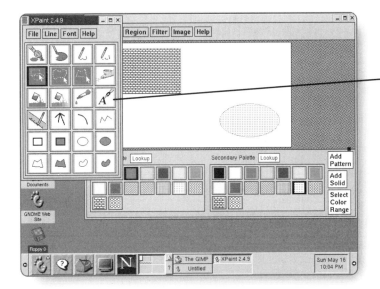

1. **Double-click** on the **Text tool** in the XPaint toolbox. The Browse and Select a Font dialog box will open.

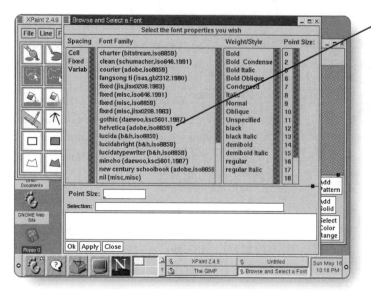

2. Click on a **font name** from the Font Family category. The Weight/Style and Point Size columns will change to reflect remaining choices.

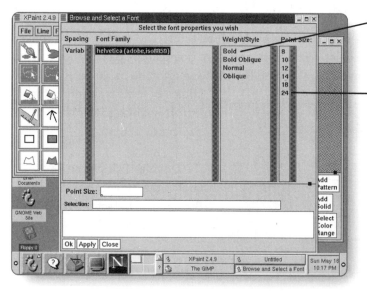

3. Click on a **font style** in the Weight/Style category. The font style will be selected.

4. Click on a **font size** in the Point Size: category. The font size will be selected and the information about the selected font and styles will appear in the Selection text box and a preview of the font will appear below it.

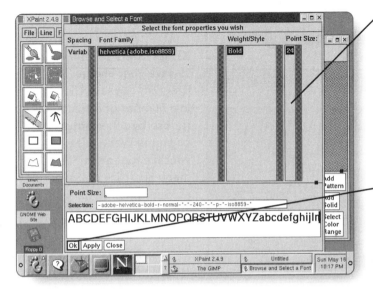

6. Click on a **blank area** in a category to see a list of choices. You can then make another selection.

7. Click on your **new selection**. Your new selection will appear in the Selection text box.

8. Click on **OK** when you are satisfied with your font selection. The Font Browser will close and the mouse pointer will change to an insertion bar when held over the canvas.

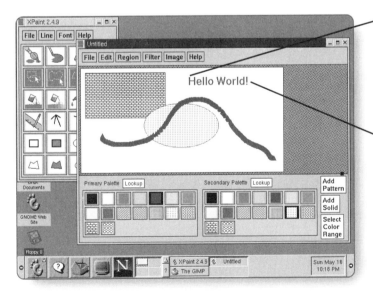

9. Click on the **place** on the canvas where you want to insert the text. A blinking cursor will appear at the text insertion point.

10. Type text. The text will appear on the canvas.

NOTE

XPaint doesn't use word wrap so you will need to press the Enter key at the end of each line. This text is a drawing element and normal text editing tools won't work. If you want to erase text, use the Erase tool.

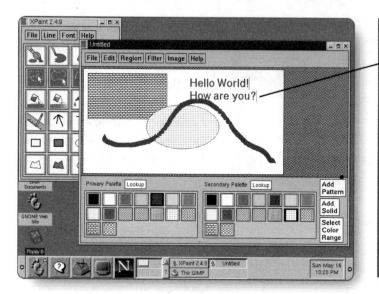

NOTE

XPaint offers several ways to save your images. The program can save the file in a number of formats for use by other programs or on the Web. To save your file, open the File menu and click on Save as. See Chapter 10, "Working with Files," if you need help saving files.

12

Getting Organized Using Linux

Linux came installed with several applications that can help you keep your personal and business life organized. Seems like there's always a checkbook to balance, invoices to tally, important dates to remember, or appointments to keep. A calculator and a calendar can come in handy. To keep track of friends, family, and business acquaintances, you'll want to keep an address book, which keeps valuable personal and business information in one place. In this chapter, you'll learn how to:

- Use the calculator
- Keep a calendar of important events
- Maintain names and addresses in the address book

Adding It up with the Calculator

Calculators are a part of everyday life. You'll need them when it's time to balance the checkbooks, work out a monthly spending budget, figure expense reports, and more.

Turning on the Calculator

The calculator is hidden beneath a number of menu layers. If you'll be using the calculator often, you may want to add an icon to the GNOME panel to find the calculator fast and easy. If you need help adding an icon, turn back to Chapter 5, "Managing Your Desktop."

1. **Click** on the **Main Menu Button**. The Main menu will appear.

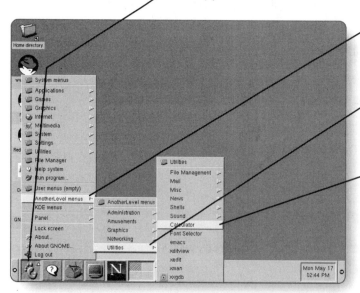

2. **Move** the **mouse pointer** to AnotherLevel menus. The AnotherLevel menu will appear.

3. **Move** the **mouse pointer** to Utilities. The AnotherLevel Utilities menu will appear.

4. **Click** on **Calculator**. The Calculator will appear on your desktop.

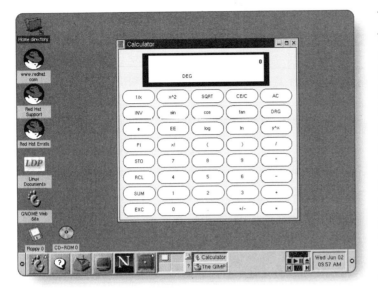

This calculator can do more than your ordinary desktop calculator. It can perform high level mathematical calculations (such as algebraic notation, logarithmic functions, financial functions, and other complex numbers). You can use this calculator as a replacement for that desktop calculator that broke. You can even use the manual that came with your now broken calculator and apply many of those instructions to this handy Linux calculator. Or, you might check out the library or used bookstore for a calculator manual.

Performing Simple Math Calculations

You might need a calculator for tasks such as adding up household budget items or balancing a checkbook. This calculator is easy to find and can help you get the job done. If you're a traveling engineer and don't want to clutter your laptop carrying case with a lot of "stuff," this calculator can perform all the calculations you'll need. Or, if you're a student on an allowance, use this calculator instead of doling out the spare cash.

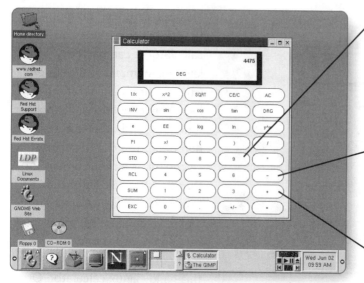

1. Click on the **number keys** that correspond with the first number in the calculation. The number will appear in the display area at the top of the calculator.

2a. Click on the **– key** if you want to subtract the next number from the first.

OR

2b. Click on the **+ key** if you want to add the next number to the first.

OR

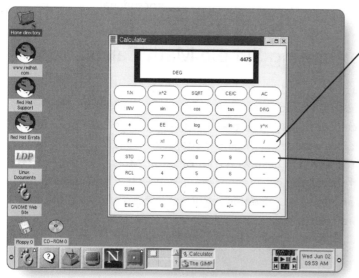

2c. Click on the **/ key** if you want to multiply the first number by the next number you'll be entering.

OR

2d. Click on the *** key** if you want to divide the first number by the next number you'll be entering.

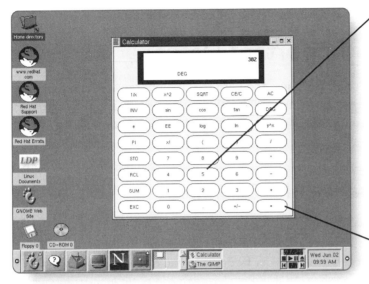

3. Click on the **number keys** that correspond with the next number in the calculation. The number will appear in the display area at the top of the calculator.

4. Add, subtract, multiply, or divide any **remaining numbers** in your calculation. The numbers will be computed in the calculation.

5. Click on the **= key**. The total for your calculation will appear in the calculator display.

NOTE

You can also use the numeric keypad on your keyboard.

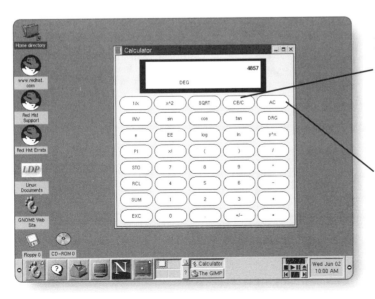

Here are a couple of tips to help you work with the Calculator:

- If you've entered the wrong number and want to clear the number (or the entry) without clearing the computation, press the CE/C key.

- If you want to clear the display so that you can start a new calculation, press the AC key.

Keeping Track of Important Dates

Some days it's just too hard to remember everything that needs to be done, all the places to be seen, and the people to meet. Keeping a calendar is the first step to organizing all these important events.

Starting the Calendar

Like the other Linux programs that you've seen throughout this book, the Calendar can be found on the Main menu. If you use the Calendar frequently, you may want to make it an icon on the GNOME Panel, or you can put it in a drawer with other important applications and files.

1. **Click** on the **Main Menu Button**. The Main Menu will appear.

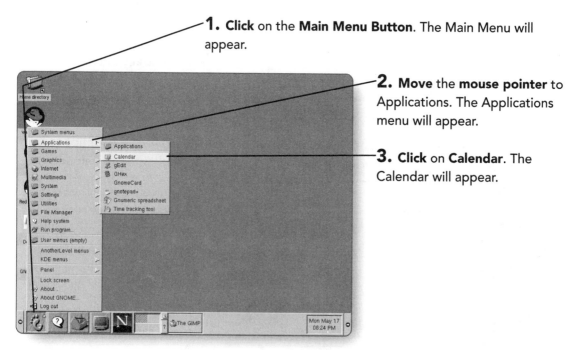

2. **Move** the **mouse pointer** to Applications. The Applications menu will appear.

3. **Click** on **Calendar**. The Calendar will appear.

Changing the Time View

When you open the calendar, you'll notice that it uses a 24-hour clock. This is great if you're in the military. Here's how to change it to a 12-hour clock. You can also change the hours that display on the calendar.

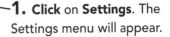
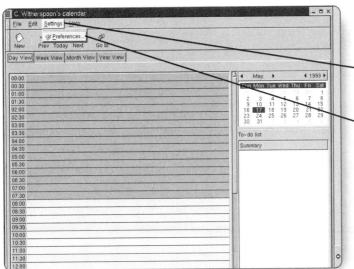

1. Click on **Settings**. The Settings menu will appear.

2. Click on **Preferences**. The Preferences dialog box will open.

3. Click on the **12-hour (AM/PM) option button**. The option will be selected.

4. Click on the **Monday option button** if you want to change the day on which the week starts. The option will be selected.

5. Click on **Apply**. You'll see the calendar change to a 12-hour format on the calendar.

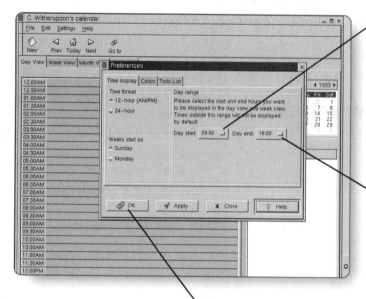

6. Click on the **Day start: list box button** and **select** the **time** (the calendar is still using a 24-hour time format to select the time) at which you want the day to start on the calendar. The time will appear in the list box.

7. Click on the **Day end: list box button** and **select** the **time** at which you want the day to end on the calendar. The time will appear in the list box.

8. Click on **OK**. Your calendar will be ready and waiting for you to fill it with appointments, reminders, and to-do lists.

Adding an Appointment

If you have a reason for being at a designated place at a certain time on a specific date, keep track of it in the calendar.

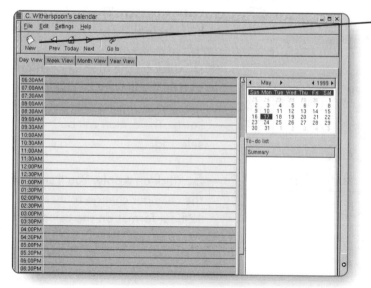

1. Click on the **New button**. The Create new appointment dialog box will open.

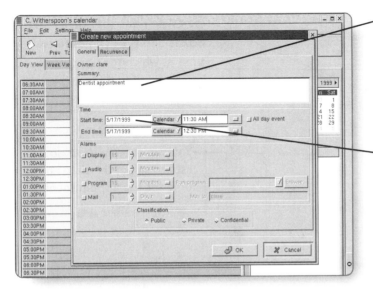

2. Click in the **Summary: text box** and **type** a **description** of the appointment, persons attending the appointment, or notes needed for the appointment.

3. Click in the **Start time: text box** and **type** the **date** on which the appointment is scheduled to begin. Use slashes (for example, mm/dd/yy).

4a. Click in the second **Start time text box** and **type** the **time** at which the appointment is scheduled.

OR

4b. Click on the **All day event check button** if you need to block out the entire day for the appointment. The option will be selected.

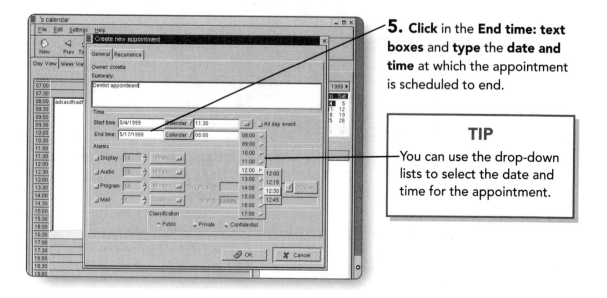

5. **Click** in the **End time: text boxes** and **type** the **date and time** at which the appointment is scheduled to end.

TIP

You can use the drop-down lists to select the date and time for the appointment.

6. Choose from a **notification option** if you want to be automatically notified in advance of an upcoming appointment.

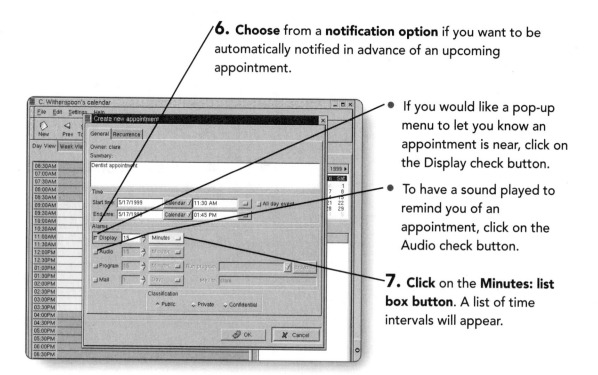

• If you would like a pop-up menu to let you know an appointment is near, click on the Display check button.

• To have a sound played to remind you of an appointment, click on the Audio check button.

7. Click on the **Minutes: list box button**. A list of time intervals will appear.

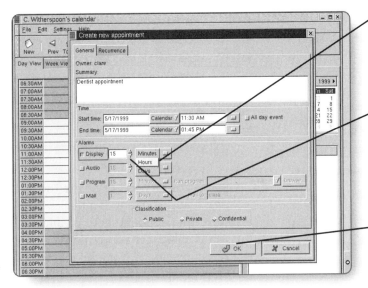

8. **Click** on the **time interval** you want to use for the notification. The interval will appear in the list box.

9. **Click** on the **up** and **down arrows** to **select** the **number** of intervals (selected in step 8) in advance that you'd like to be reminded of the appointment.

10. **Click** on **OK**. The appointment will be added to your calendar.

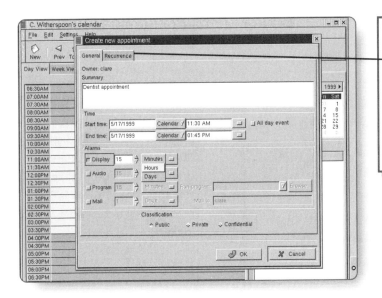

TIP

If this appointment will be a regular occurrence, click on the Recurrence tab and set up the appointment so that it is repeated in the calendar.

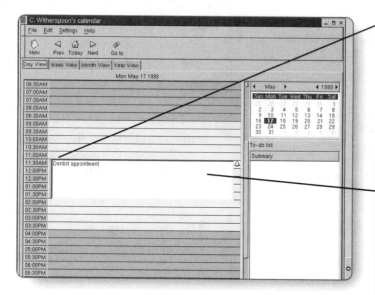

Your appointment will appear in a box on the Day View of the calendar. If you added a notification alarm to the appointment, a bell icon will be to the right of the appointment box.

TIP

You can edit or delete the appointment. Right-click on the appointment box and select the appropriate command from the menu that appears.

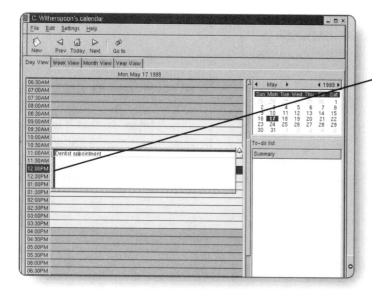

Here's a few tips for editing appointments:

- To move an appointment to a different time during the same day, click inside the appointment box to display the box outline. Click and drag the left side outline until the appointment box is moved to the desired location.

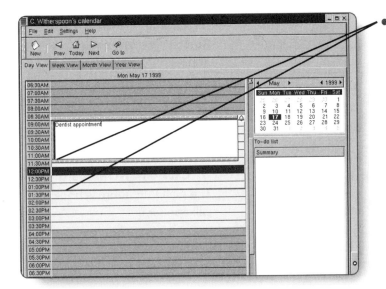

● To change the time span for an appointment, click inside the appointment box to display the box outline. Click and drag the top outline to move the start time or click and drag the bottom outline to move the end time.

Maintaining an Address Book

The GNOME address book is the electronic equivalent of a card file or the little black book you keep in your wallet. But, it is much more sophisticated. Along with being able to store information about friends, family, and business associates, you can sort and view addresses in a variety of ways.

Opening the Address Book

Use the GNOME address book to keep track of your contacts. Taking the time now to learn about the address book features will make the job of maintaining it a snap.

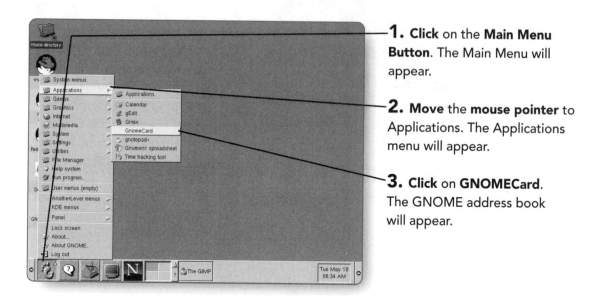

1. **Click** on the **Main Menu Button**. The Main Menu will appear.

2. **Move** the **mouse pointer** to Applications. The Applications menu will appear.

3. **Click** on **GNOMECard**. The GNOME address book will appear.

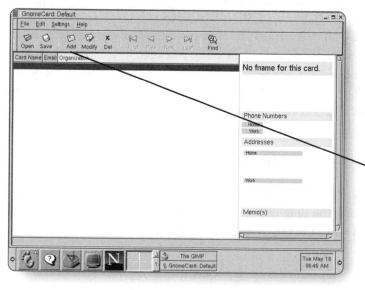

Adding an Address

Adding new names and addresses to the address book is as simple as clicking on a button and typing information into a dialog box.

1. **Click** on the **Add button**. The gnomecard dialog box will open.

2. Type the **full name** of your contact in the First, Middle, and Last: text boxes.

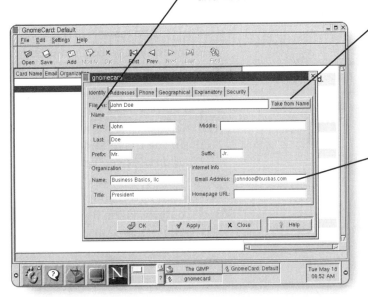

3. Click on the **Take from Name button**. The contact's name will appear in the File As: text box. This is how you will see the contact's name listed in the list of addresses.

4. Type the **e-mail address** for the contact in the Email Address: text box.

5. Fill in other **fields** as needed.

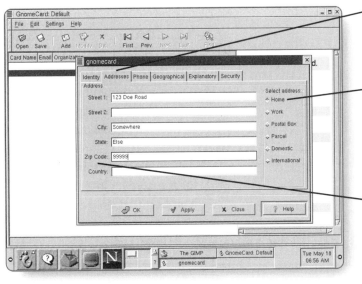

6. Click on the **Addresses tab**. The Addresses tab will come to the top of the stack.

7. Click on an **option button** in the Select address section that corresponds to the type of address you want to enter for the contact.

8. Type the street and city **information** for the contact in the corresponding text boxes.

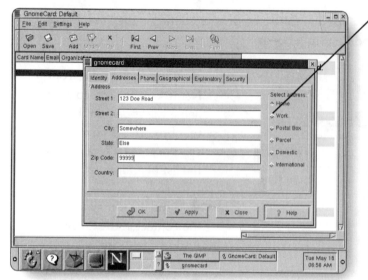

9. Click on a different **option button** to add another address in the Select address section. The text boxes will all become blank for you to add the other address information.

NOTE

To see the different addresses you've entered for the contact, click on each of the option buttons in the Select address section.

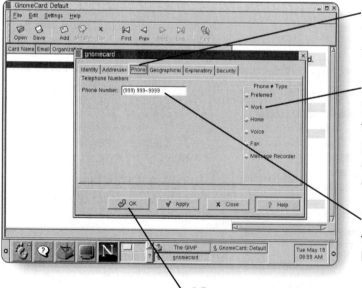

10. Click on the **Phone tab**. The Phone tab will come to the top of the stack.

11. Click on an **option button** in the Phone # Type: section that corresponds to the type of phone number you will be adding for the contact. The option will be selected.

12. Type the **phone number** for the contact in the Phone Number: text box.

13. Click on **OK**. The contact will appear in the address book.

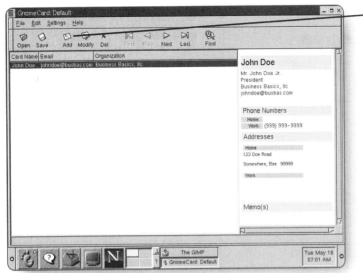

14. **Add** other **contacts** as needed. The contact will appear in the address list.

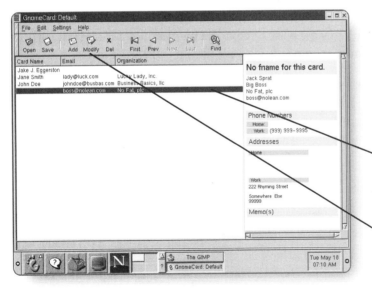

Updating Address Information

If you need to make changes to a person's address listing, just follow these easy steps.

1. **Click** on the **contact** whose information you want to change. The contact will be selected.

2. **Click** on the **Modify button**. The gnomecard dialog box with the selected contact's address information will open.

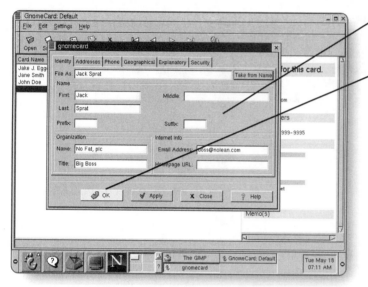

3. Make the necessary **changes** or **additions**.

4. Click on **OK**. The contact's information will be updated.

Sorting Addresses

You can view a list of contacts by name, e-mail address, or company name.

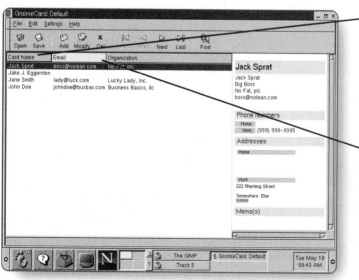

1. Click on the **Card Name column heading**. The list of contacts will be sorted by the name you used as the card name and will display in alphabetical order.

2. Click on the **Email column heading**. The list of contacts will be sorted by e-mail address in alphabetical order.

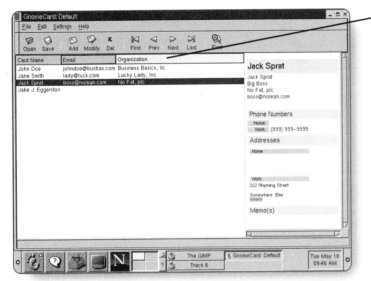

3. Click on the **Organization column heading**. The list of contacts will be sorted by the contacts' company names in alphabetical order.

Adding Column Headings

You can add additional column headings to the contacts' list. Look through the list of column headings to see which ones will help you work with your address list easier.

1. Click on **Settings**. The Settings menu will appear.

2. Click on **Preferences**. The gnomecard dialog box will appear.

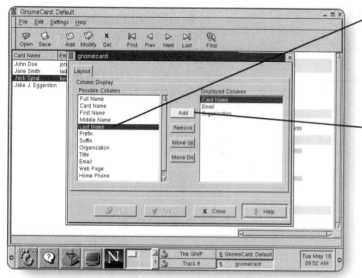

3. Scroll through the **Possible Columns list** and **click** on a **column heading** that you want to add to the list. The column heading will be selected.

4. Click on **Add**. The column heading will be added to the bottom of the Displayed Columns list. You can also change the order of the column headings.

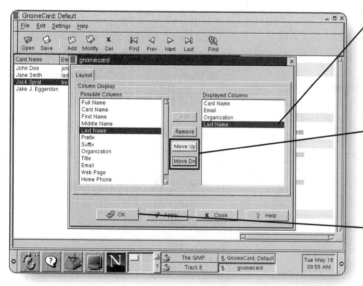

5. Click on the **column heading** in the Displayed Columns list that you want to move. The column heading will be selected.

6. Click on the **Move Up or Move Dn button**. The position of the column will be moved in the list.

7. Click on **OK**. The dialog box will close and your changes will be made.

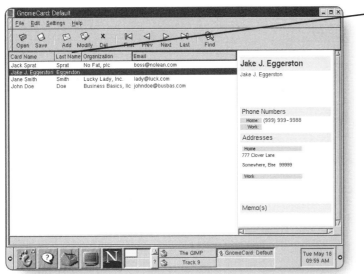

You'll see the new column headings and the reordered columns.

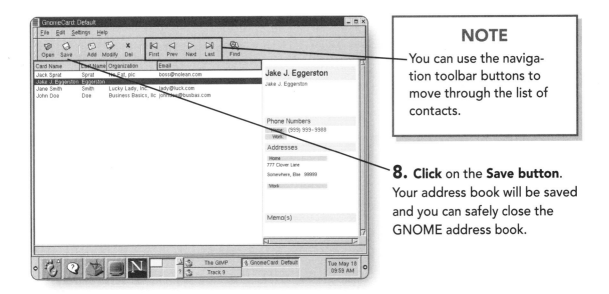

NOTE

You can use the navigation toolbar buttons to move through the list of contacts.

8. Click on the **Save button**. Your address book will be saved and you can safely close the GNOME address book.

13

Printing Files

Because Linux is a multi-user/multi-tasking operating system, it offers many benefits to the user not found in single-user operating systems. One of the biggest benefits is the printing system. Printing in Linux is more feature-rich, flexible, and different than printing in a DOS or Windows environment. Linux uses an easily configurable spooling subsystem to control printing. The system enables printing to any printer available. It can be a local (attached) printer, a printer attached to another Linux machine, a network printer, or even a Windows 95/98/NT network printer. In this chapter, you'll learn how to:

- Set up a printer that is attached to your computer
- Print files using drag and drop

Configuring a Local Printer

The Red Hat Printer Tool provides a graphical front-end for the Linux PrintTool applet and will help you to set up a printer. It provides some of the information automatically, and lets you select the rest from easy graphical menus. To access the Red Hat Linux Print System Manager, you must first log in as superuser or root.

Setting Up the Printer

1. **Click** on the **Main Menu Button**. The Main Menu will appear.

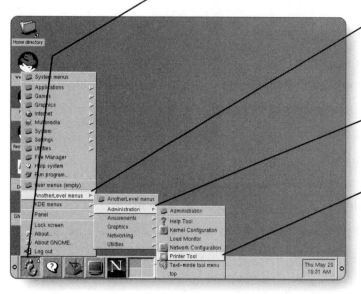

2. **Move** the **mouse pointer** to AnotherLevel menus. The AnotherLevel menus listing will appear.

3. **Click** on **Administration**. The Administration menu will appear.

4. **Click** on **Printer Tool**. The Red Hat Linux Print System Manager will appear.

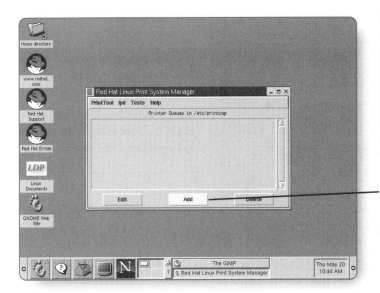

NOTE

You may see a series of Error dialog boxes. Press OK to skip these messages and continue to the printer tool.

5. Click on **Add**. The Add a Printer Entry dialog box will open.

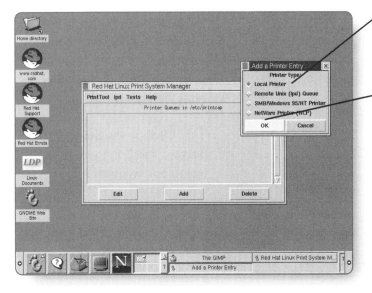

6. Click on the **Local Printer option button**. The option will be selected.

7. Click on **OK**. An Info dialog box will open showing the list of auto-detected printer ports.

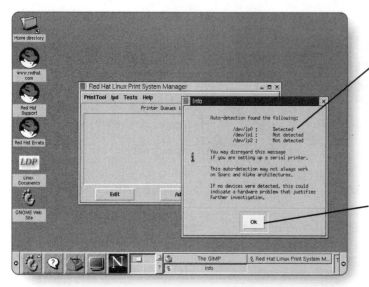

NOTE

Linux numbers parallel ports differently than DOS. If Linux detected lp0, it is equivalent to lpt1 in DOS. Following that, lp1=lpt2 and lp2=lpt3.

8. **Click** on **OK**. The Edit Local Printer Entry dialog box will open.

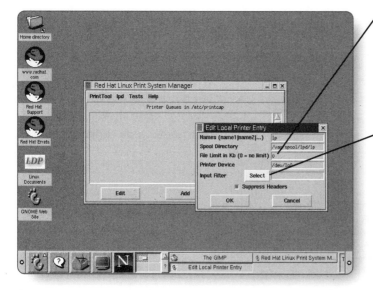

9. **Click** in the **text box** next to File Limit in Kb to limit the size files that your user accounts can send to the printer and then **type** the **number** of Kb.

10. **Click** on the **Select button**. The Configure Filter dialog box will open.

NOTE

Many printers emulate other printers. If your printer is on the list, select it; if not, try and find one that closely matches it.

11. **Click** on a **printer** in the Printer Type list. The printer will be selected and the right panel will display details for the printer driver.

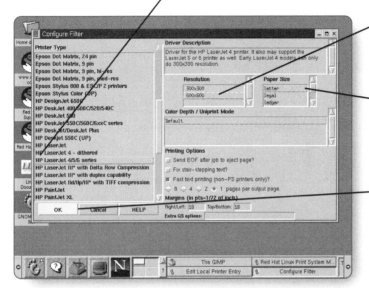

12. **Click** on a **resolution** for the default print resolution. The resolution will be selected.

13. **Click** on the **paper size** you will be using most of the time. The paper size will be selected.

14. **Click** on **OK**. You will be taken back to the Edit Local Printer Entry dialog box.

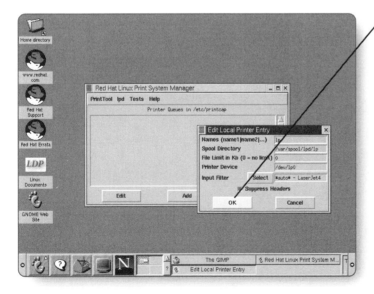

15. **Click** on **OK**. The dialog box will close and you'll return to the Print System Manager.

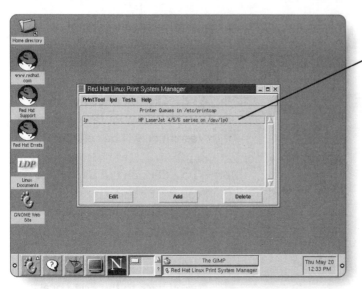

Testing the Printer

1. Click on the **printer** you just added. The printer will be selected.

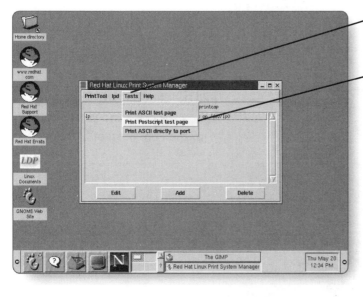

2. Click on the **Tests menu**. The Test menu will appear.

3. Click on **Print Postscript test page**. An Info dialog box will open telling you that the test page has been sent to the printer queue and a test page will print.

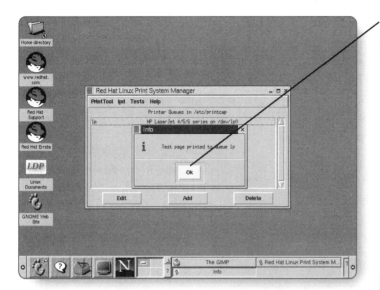

4. Click on **OK**. The Info dialog box will close and you'll return to the Print System Manager.

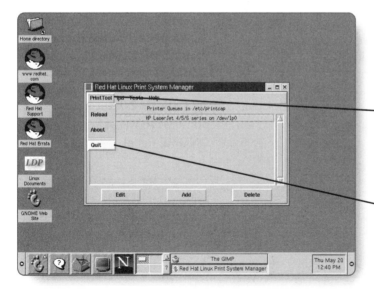

5. Click on the **PrintTool menu** when you are satisfied with the result. The PrintTool menu will appear.

6. Click on **Quit**. The PrintTool utility will close. Now, your user accounts are ready to use the printer.

Printing Files

Now that the system knows that you have a printer, all users will have access to it. Before they can have access to the printer, they'll need to add a printer applet to their GNOME Panel. Once they have the applet, it's a matter of drag and drop to print a file.

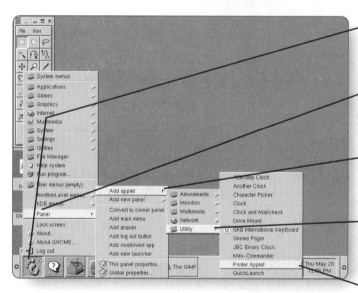

1. Click on the **Main Menu Button**. The Main Menu will appear.

2. Move the **mouse pointer** to Panel. The Panel menu will appear.

3. Move the **mouse pointer** to Add Applet. The Add Applet menu will appear.

4. Move the **mouse pointer** to Utility. The Utility menu will appear.

5. Click on **Printer Applet**. A printer icon will appear on the GNOME Panel.

Your printer is now ready. To print, open the file manager, drag the file that you want to print over the top of the icon and drop the file. After a few moments, it will print.

14

Sounding Off with Your Computer

If you have a multimedia computer (that is, a computer with speakers, a CD-ROM drive, and a sound card), you can make your computer play a variety of sounds. You can set alarms and warning bells to let you know you performed a certain event or made a mistake. If you have a music CD collection, you can enjoy listening to music while you work at your computer. In this chapter, you'll learn how to:

- Set a different sound for the keyboard bell
- Change the system event sounds
- Play your music collection on the CD player

Setting System Sounds

You may have heard your computer make a number of beeping, clanging, buzzing, and popping sounds. No, your computer isn't falling apart. These sounds are telling you that you performed a certain event, or that you made an error. Depending on where your computer is located and your personal preferences, you may want to change the sounds your computer makes.

Changing the Keyboard Bell

The keyboard bell is actually a warning that a keyboard input was made in error. Experiment with the tone of the bell until you find a sound you like. You can make your keyboard bell a tenor or a baritone.

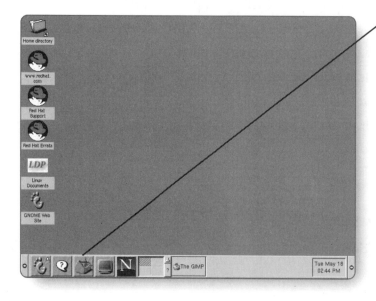

1. **Click** on the **GNOME Control Center icon** on the GNOME Panel. The Control Center window will open.

2. Click on **Keyboard Bell**. The Keyboard Bell panel will appear in the right pane of the Control Center window.

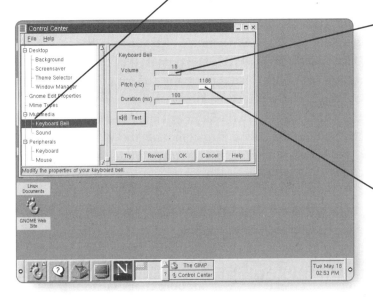

3. Click and **drag** the **Volume slider** to change the volume of the bell that sounds when a keyboard error is made. Dragging the slider to the left will turn the volume down. Dragging the slider to the right will turn the volume up.

4. Click and **drag** the **Pitch slider** to change the musical note that plays. Dragging the slider to the left will play a lower key. Dragging the slider to the right will play a higher key.

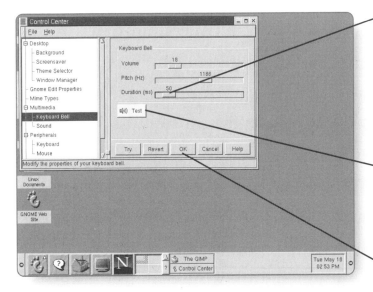

5. Click and **drag** the **Duration slider** to change the amount of time you hear the keyboard sound. Dragging the slider to the left plays a shorter sound. Dragging the slider to the right plays a longer sound.

6. Click on the **Test button**. You'll hear how your changes affect the sound of the keyboard bell.

7. Click on **OK**. Your changes will be applied.

Changing Sound Events

You can change the sounds your computer makes when you perform such tasks such as executing menu commands or logging out of GNOME. There are also sound events associated with the various Linux games. If all the noise is getting to you, you can turn off the sounds completely. If you don't hear any sounds, it may be because your sound card is not compatible with Red Hat Linux. You can find out by reading the sound card compatibility Web page at www.redhat.com/corp/support/hardware/intel/60/rh6.0-hcl-i.ld-13.html.

1. **Click** on **Sound**. The Sound pane will appear on the right side of the Control Center window.

2. **Click** on the **GNOME sound support check button**. The option will be selected.

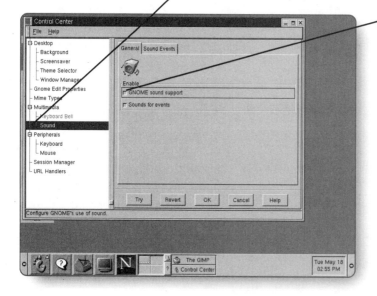

3. Click on the **Sound Events tab**. The Sound Events tab will come to the top of the stack.

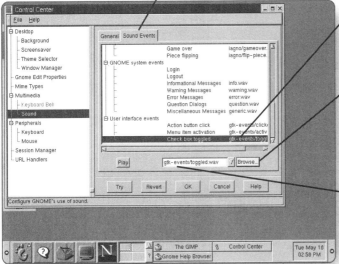

4. Click on the **sound event** that you want to change. The sound event will be highlighted.

5. Click on the **Browse button**. The Select sound file dialog box will open.

NOTE

If you don't want a sound associated with an event, delete the directory path and file name in the text box.

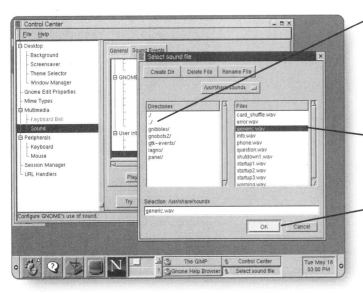

6. Click on **../** in the Directories list to change to a different directory that contains a WAV sound that you can use. The directory will be changed.

7. Click on the **sound file** that you want to use for the sound event. The file will be selected.

8. Click on **OK**. The new sound will appear next to the event you selected.

9. Click on the **Play button**. You'll hear the sound you selected.

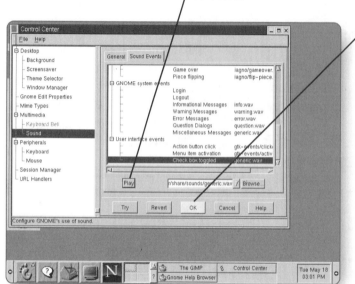

10. Click on **OK**. Your changes will be made.

Tuning Up with the CD Player

If your computer has a CD-ROM drive, a sound card, and speakers, you can play music CDs while you work at your computer. Not only can you just listen to the CD in the order the tracks appear on the CD, but you can also switch between tracks.

Starting the CD Player

It's time to play a few tunes, so get your favorite music CD ready and crank up the jukebox.

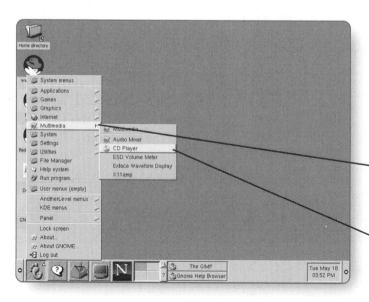

1. Click on the **Main Menu Button**. The Main Menu will appear.

2. Move the **mouse pointer** to Multimedia. The Multimedia menu will appear.

3. Click on **CD Player**. The CD player will appear on your desktop.

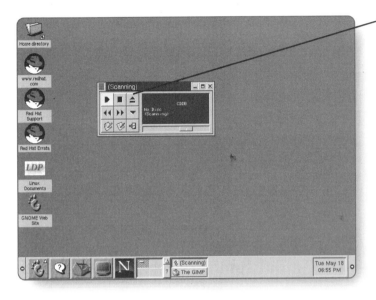

4. Click on the **Eject button**. The CD carriage for your CD-ROM drive will slide out of the computer.

5. Place the **music CD** in the CD carriage.

6. Click on the **Eject button** on your computer's CD-ROM drive. The carriage will close.

Playing Music CDs

Now that you have a CD in the CD-ROM drive and the CD player turned on, it's time to learn how to use the CD player.

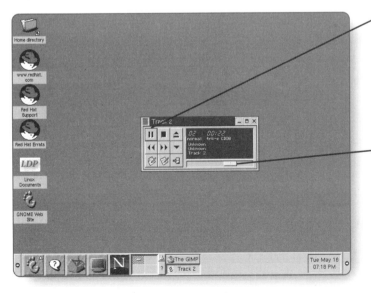

1. Click on the **Play button**. You'll begin to hear music come from your computer speakers. Notice that the button changes. Click on this button a second time to pause the song.

2. Click and **drag** on the **Volume slider**. Dragging the slider to the right will make the music louder. Dragging the slider to the left will turn the volume down.

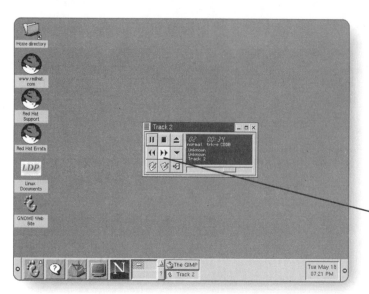

3. Click on the **Skip forwards button**. The song that is playing will stop and the next song on the CD play list will begin playing.

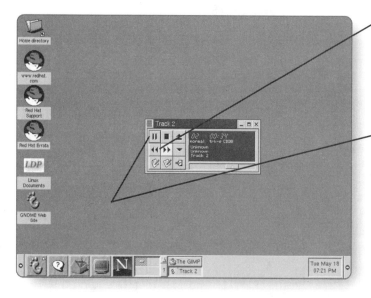

4. Click on the **Skip backwards button**. The song that is playing will stop and the previous song on the CD play list will begin playing.

5. Click on the **Pause button**. The music will stop playing but the CD player will remember where it left off.

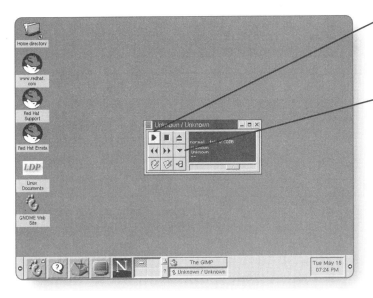

6. Click on the **Play button**. The CD will begin playing at the place where it was paused.

7. Click on the **Track Selection button**. A list of the track numbers on the CD will appear.

8. Click on the **track** that you want to listen to. The selected track will begin playing.

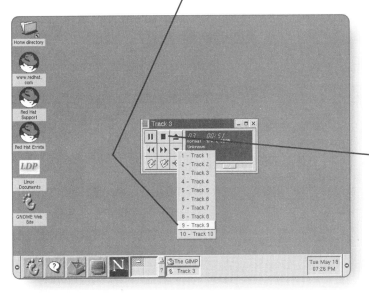

NOTE

The number of tracks corresponds to the number of songs on the CD.

9. Click on the **Stop button** when you're finished listening to the CD. The music will stop.

Keeping a Play List for Your Favorite CDs

The CD player will keep a list of songs that appear on a CD. You'll need to supply the information, but you'll be able to see this information each time you put that CD in the CD player. You won't need to keep going back to the album cover to find the song list.

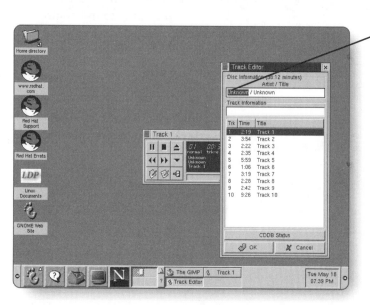

1. Click on the **Open Track Editor button**. The Track Editor dialog box will open.

NOTE

Before you begin, make sure the CD is in the CD-ROM drive and that you have the album jacket with the song list in front of you.

2. Double-click on the first occurrence of the word **Unknown** in the Artist/Title text box. The word will be selected.

3. Type the **name** of the singer or band appearing on the CD.

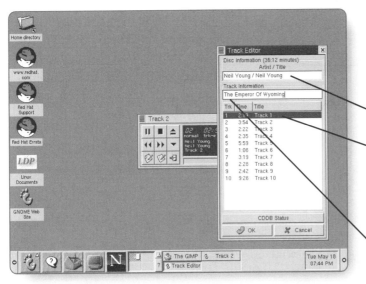

4. Double-click on the second occurrence of the word **Unknown** in the Artist/Title text box. The word will be selected.

5. Type the **title** of the CD.

6. Click on the **track number** in the Track List to which you want to add a song title. The track number will be selected.

7. Type the **title** of the song that corresponds to that track.

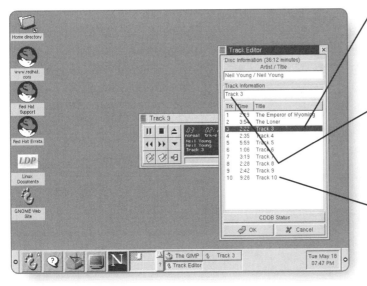

8. Click on the **next track** to which you want to add a song title. The track number will be selected.

9. Clear any **text** that may appear in the Track Information text box and type the song title of the corresponding track.

10. Add song titles to the other tracks on the CD. The entire play list will be added to the Track Editor.

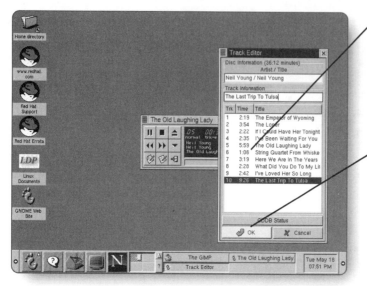

11. **Look over** the **play list** and make sure you didn't make any typing mistakes. If you did, click on the track that contains the error and fix it in the Track Information text box.

12. **Click** on **OK** when you are finished. The Track Editor will close.

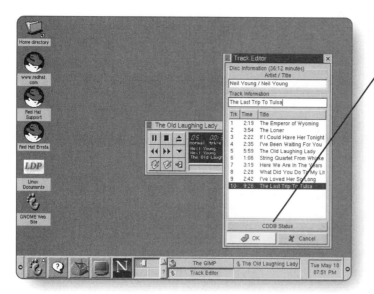

TIP

If you have Internet access, you may not need to type in all this information. Connect to your Internet service provider and click on the CDDB Status button. If the album is in the database, all the information will be filled in for you.

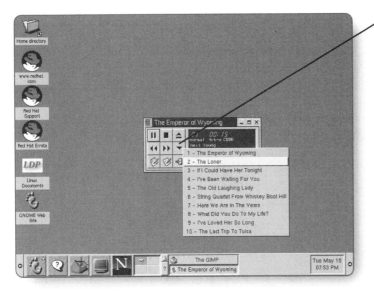

13. **Click** on the **Track Selection button**. A play list will appear showing the titles of each song on each track.

These titles will still be there after you take the CD out of the CD-ROM drive and turn off the CD player. Next time you play this CD, the artist, album title, and play list will display automatically.

Playing CDs Automatically

You may have noticed that the CD did not start playing automatically when you closed the CD carriage. You can change this.

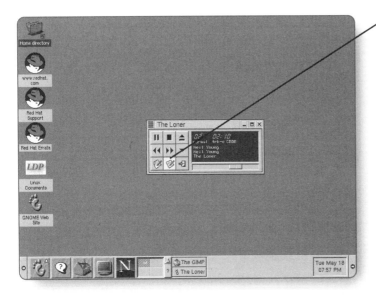

1. **Click** on the **Preferences button**. The Preferences dialog box will open.

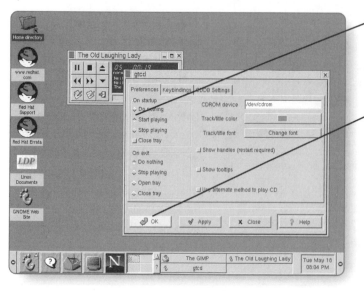

2. Click on the **Start playing option button** in the On startup area. The option will be selected.

3. Click on **OK**. The next time you put a CD in the CD-ROM drive, the CD player will begin playing the first song.

Changing the Look of the CD Player

The CD player display shows you the artist, album title, song title, and track number for the CD that is currently playing. If the default text style and color are hard for you to read, you can change the appearance of the CD player.

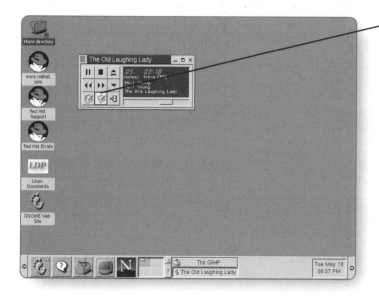

1. Click on the **Preferences button**. The Preferences dialog box will open.

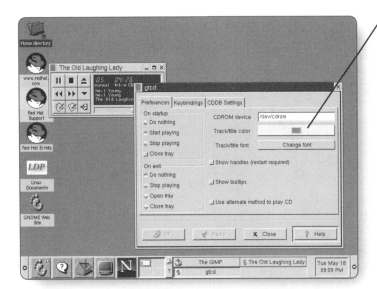

2. Click on the **Track/title color button**. The Pick a color dialog box will open.

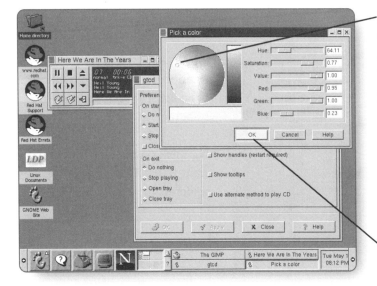

3a. Click on the small **circle** in the color wheel and **drag** it **around** on the wheel. The color in the Match tile will change as you drag the circle.

OR

3b. Click on any part of the **color wheel**. The color in the Match tile will change to your choice.

4. Click on **OK**. The color will appear in the Track/title color button.

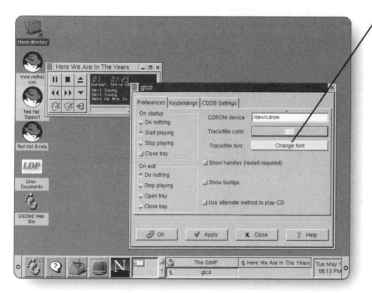

5. Click on the **Track/title font button**. The Font dialog box will open.

6. Click on the **font** in the Font list that you want to use on the CD display. The font will be selected.

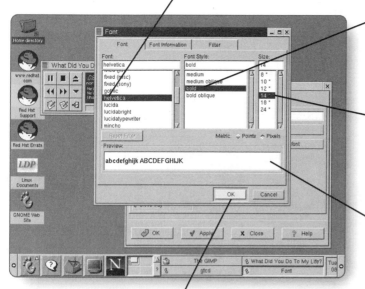

7. Click on the **style** you want to apply to the font in the Font Style list. The font style will be selected.

8. Click on the **size** font you want to use. The size will be selected

NOTE

You'll see a preview of the font in the Preview area.

9. Click on **OK**. The Font dialog box will close and you'll return to the Preferences dialog box.

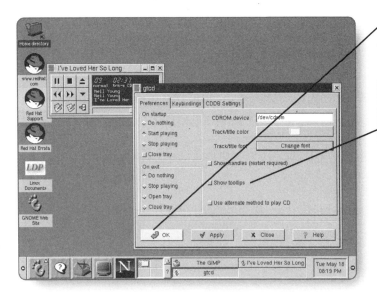

10. **Click** on **OK**. Your changes will be made to the CD display.

TIP

You can turn the tooltips for the CD player on and off by clicking on the Show tooltips check button.

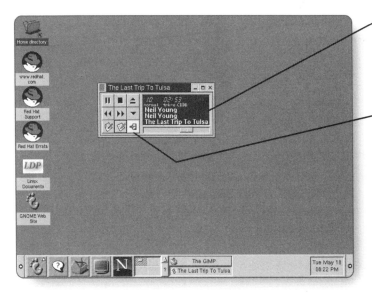

The display will show the artist, album title, and currently playing song in the new font and color that you selected.

11. **Click** on the **Exit button** when you are finished playing the CD player. The CD player will close.

Part III Review Questions

1. What menu in an application normally contains the command that saves files? *See "Creating a New File" in Chapter 10*

2. What are three different methods of selecting text? *See "Working with Text" in Chapter 10*

3. How do you create a new canvas in XPaint on which to place your drawings? *See "Getting Started with XPaint" in Chapter 11*

4. What tool do you use in the toolbox to move an object you've created on the XPaint canvas? *See "Creating Great Graphics with XPaint" in Chapter 11*

5. Where can you find a Linux program that will help you keep your appointments organized? *See "Keeping Track of Important Dates" in Chapter 12*

6. How do you add a new address listing to the GNOME address book? *See "Maintaining an Address Book" in Chapter 12*

7. Where do you find the print tool that configures a printer for you? *See "Configuring a Local Printer" in Chapter 13*

8. How do you place an icon on the GNOME Panel so that you can easily print files? *See "Printing Files" in Chapter 13*

9. What are the two types of system sounds that you can change for your computer? *See "Setting System Sounds" in Chapter 14*

10. How do you keep a play list in the CD Player? *See "Tuning Up with the CD Player" in Chapter 14*

PART IV

Tuning Up Your Linux

15

Managing Disk Drives

In Chapter 9, "Maintaining Your Linux," you learned how to mount a floppy disk so that you could create a recovery disk set. These recovery disks are a must for every Linux repair kit. Chances are that your CD-ROM drive was already mounted. Linux should do this automatically during the installation. If you want to do more with CDs than just play music, you'll need to make sure the CD-ROM drive is mounted and then you can browse the contents of the CD. You may also want to know more about working with floppy drives, other than just how to mount them. In this chapter, you'll learn how to:

- Set up a CD-ROM drive for your Linux system
- Give users on the system the ability to read CDs
- Format a floppy disk
- Read from and write to a floppy disk

Configuring the CD-ROM Drive

Chances are that when you installed Linux, the installation detected your CD-ROM drive. If you're having problems using your CD-ROM drive, run through these steps to make sure everything is set up so that all the users on the system can access the CD-ROM drive. You must be logged in as the superuser or root before you can mount the CD-ROM drive.

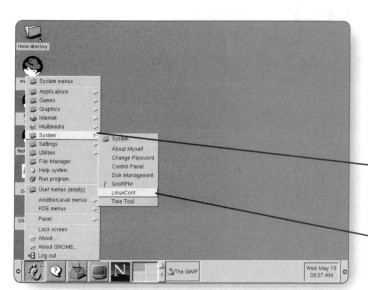

1. Click on the **Main Menu button**. The Main Menu will appear.

2. Move the **mouse pointer** to System. The System menu will appear.

3. Click on **LinuxConf**. The LinuxConf configuration utility will open.

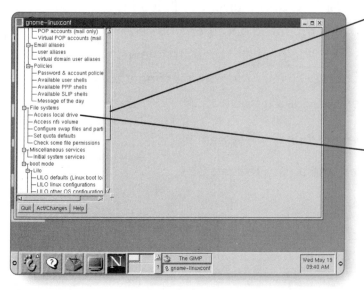

4. Scroll down the **Configuration list** until the File systems section is showing. The list of File system configuration options will appear.

5. Click on **Access local drive**. The Local volume pane will appear.

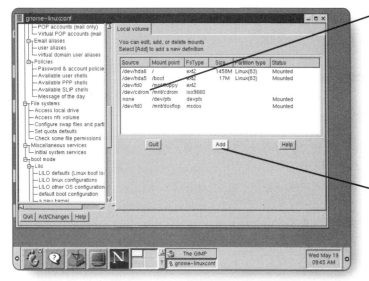

6a. **Click** on **/dev/cdrom** if you have a listing for it in the Source column. The Volume specification pane will appear. Make sure that the information for your CD-ROM matches the following steps.

OR

6b. **Click** on the **Add button** if you do not have the listing in the Source column. The Volume specification pane will appear. You'll need to add the information in the following steps.

7. **Click** in the **Partition text box.** The insertion point will be in the text box.

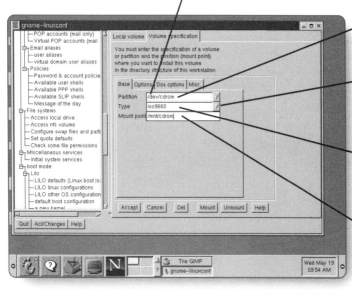

8. **Type /dev/cdrom.** The text will appear in the text box.

9. **Click** on the **down arrow** next to the Type list box. A drop-down list will appear.

10. **Click** on **iso9660** to select it. The type will appear in the list box.

11. **Click** in the **text box** next to Mount point and **type /mnt/cdrom**.

12. **Click** on the **Options tab**. The Options tab will come to the top of the stack.

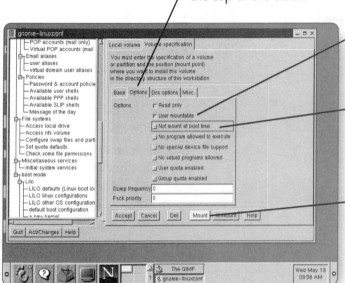

13. **Click** on the **check button** next to User mountable. The option will be selected.

14. **Click** on the **check button** next to Not mount at boot time if it is not selected. The option will be selected.

15. **Click** on the **Mount button**. The Mount file system pane will appear.

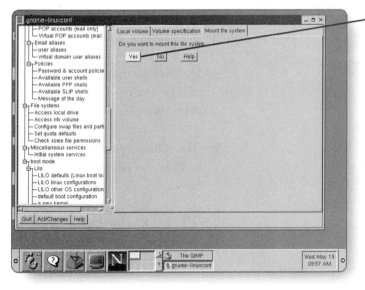

16. **Click** on the **Yes button**. The Please note pane will appear.

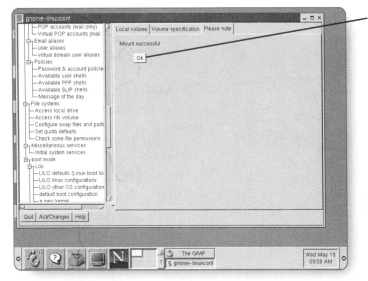

17. **Click** on the **OK button**. You will return to the Volume specification pane.

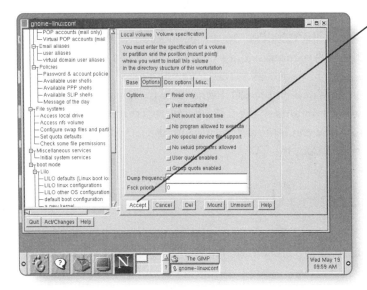

18. **Click** on the **Accept button**. The changes will be applied to the system and you will return to the Local volume pane.

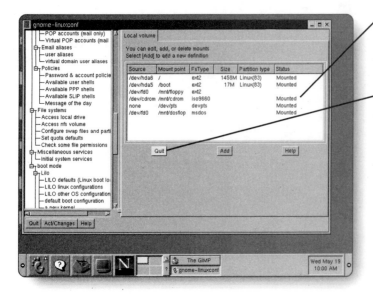

You'll notice that CD-ROM drive is listed and that the status is shown as mounted.

19. **Click** on the **Quit button**. The Local volume pane will close.

NOTE

Click on the Kill button to close the Linuxconf configuration utility.

Working with CDs

Now that the CD-ROM drive is configured so that your Linux system will recognize it, it's time to mount the drive so that users can have access to the drive, read its contents, and use files contained on the CD. Remember that before you can view the contents of the CD, you must first mount it. And, before you can remove the CD from the CD-ROM drive, you must unmount the CD.

Mounting the CD

Before you can use a CD, make sure that the CD-drive is mounted in your user account.

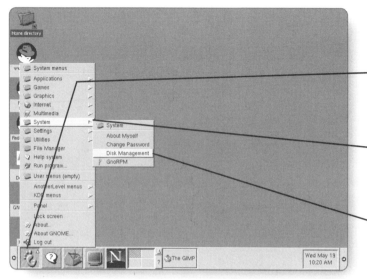

1. Place the **CD** in the CD-ROM Drive.

2. Click on the **Main Menu button**. The Main Menu will appear.

3. Move the **mouse pointer** to System. The System menu will appear.

4. Click on **Disk Management**. The User Mount Tool utility will open.

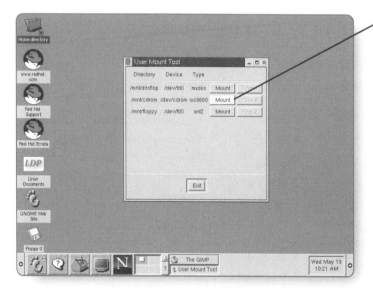

5. Click on the **Mount button** located to the right of the /mnt/cdrom directory. The button will change to Unmount and the CD-ROM drive will be mounted so that the user can have access to it.

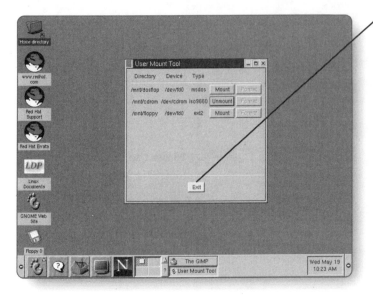

6. Click on **Exit**. The User Mount Tool utility will close and the user will have access to the CD-ROM drive.

Browsing the Contents of the CD-ROM

You've got a CD in the CD-ROM drive and the drive is mounted. Now you're ready to see what's on the CD.

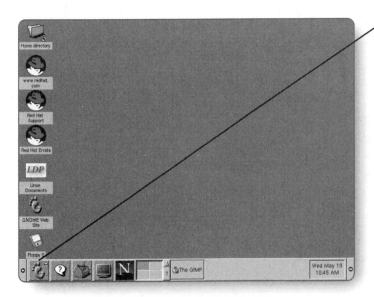

1. Double-click on the **Home directory icon**. The File Manager will open and your user home directory will be displayed.

NOTE

If you don't have this icon on your desktop, open the Main Menu and click on File Manager.

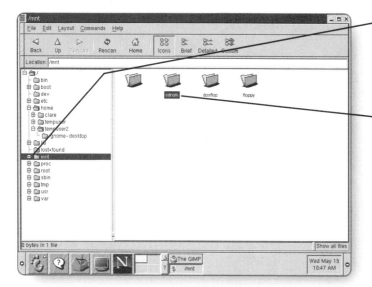

2. Double click on the **/mnt directory**. The list of devices that are available on the system will appear.

3. Double click on the **/cdrom directory**. The list of files and directories contained on the CD will appear.

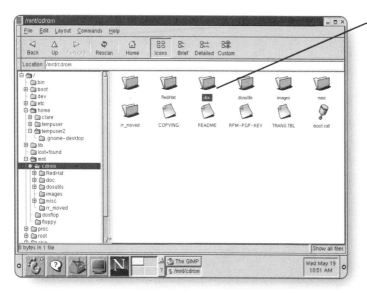

4. Double-click on a **subdirectory** on the CD. The list of files contained in that directory will appear.

5. Double-click on **subdirectories** until you see the files for which you are looking. The files contained in the directory will appear.

Reading Files on a CD

Now that you've displayed the file that you want to read, you may need to tell Linux which application you'll want to use to open the file.

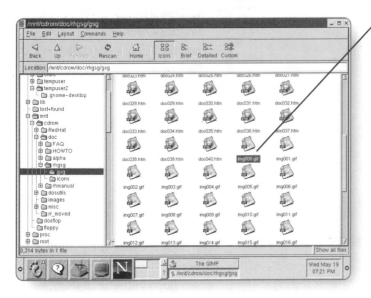

1. Double-click on the **file** that you want to open. One of two things will happen. Either the file will open in the program associated with it or the gmc dialog box will open where you can select an application with which to read the file.

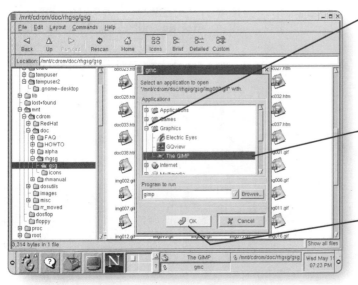

2. Click on the **plus sign** in the gmc dialog box next to the menu that contains the application you want to use to open the file.

3. Click on the **application**. The application will be selected and the program name will appear in the Program to run text box.

4. Click on **OK**. The file will open in the selected application.

Ejecting the CD

Unmount the drive before you remove the CD from the CD-ROM drive.

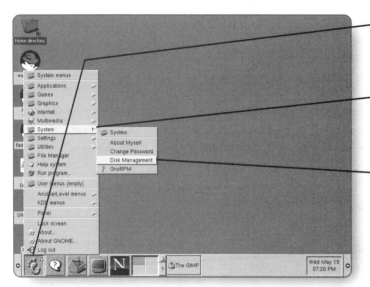

1. Click on the **Main Menu button**. The Main Menu will appear.

2. Move the **mouse pointer** to System. The System menu will appear

3. Click on **Disk Management**. The User Mount Tool utility will open.

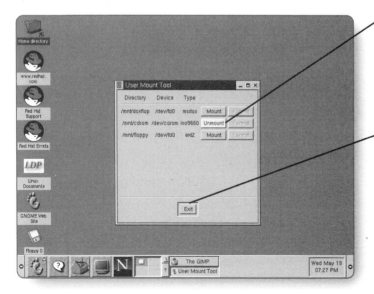

4. Click on the **Unmount button** for the /mnt/cdrom directory. The CD-ROM drive will be unmounted and the button will change to Mount.

5. Click on **Exit**. The CD-ROM drive will be unmounted.

6. Press the **Eject button** on the CD-ROM drive. You'll be able to remove the CD from the drive.

Working with Floppy Disks

It's amazing that the floppy disk is still a regular part of this high tech world. Even with e-mail, high capacity backup media, and network file sharing, files still get passed around on a floppy disk.

Formatting a Floppy Disk

Before you can use a floppy disk on the Linux file system, it needs to be formatted. Linux can read a DOS formatted floppy, and it can format the disk in the DOS format.

1. **Click** on the **Main Menu Button**. The Main Menu will appear.

2. **Move** the **mouse pointer** to System. The System menu will appear.

3. **Click** on **Disk Management**. The User Mount Tool utility will open.

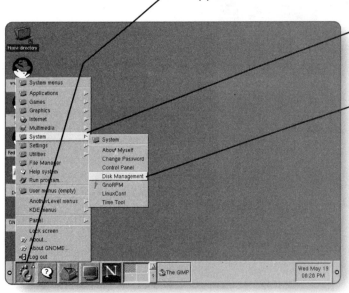

4. **Place** a **floppy disk** in your computer's floppy disk drive.

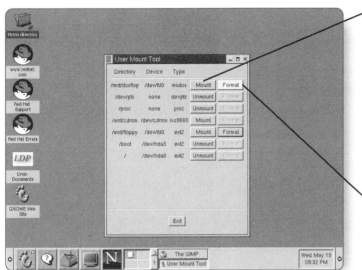

5. **Click** on the **Unmount button,** if the disk is mounted, for either the msdos (DOS and Windows) or the ext2 (Linux file system), depending on which type of format you want to perform. Note that this is a toggle button, and switches between Mount and Unmount.

6. **Click** on the **Format button**. The Confirm dialog box will open.

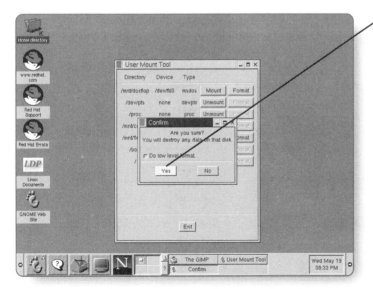

7. **Click** on **Yes**. Linux will begin formatting the disk in the type selected. When the format is finished, you are ready to copy files to the disk.

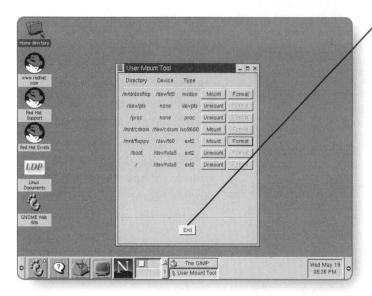

8. Click on the **Exit button** when the format is complete. The User Mount Tool utility will close.

Copying Files to a Floppy Disk

You can use the drag and drop technique to copy files from your home directory to the floppy disk drive. Before you begin, place the floppy disk into the floppy disk drive and mount the drive.

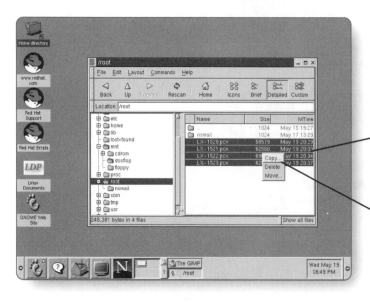

1. Click on the **Home Directory icon**. The File Manager will open and your home directory will be displayed.

2. Select the **files** that you want to copy to the floppy drive. The files will be selected.

3. Right-click on the selected **files** and **click** on **Copy**. The Copy dialog box will open.

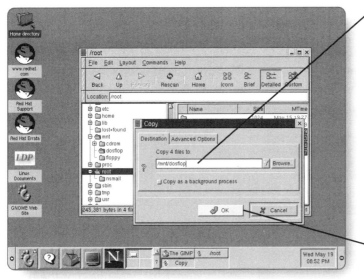

4a. Type a **destination** in the Copy 4 files to: text box. Type /mnt/dosflop if you will be copying to a DOS formatted disk.

OR

4b. Type a **destination.** Type /mnt/floppy if you will be copying to a Linux formatted disk.

5. **Click** on **OK**. The files will be moved to the directory you selected and will then be copied onto the floppy disk.

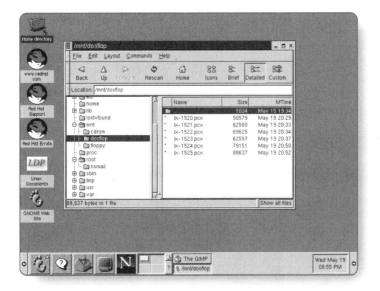

NOTE

Before you take the floppy disk out of the floppy disk drive, unmount the drive.

Reading a Floppy Disk

Linux allows you to read the contents of either a Linux-formatted floppy or a DOS-formatted floppy. Begin by putting the disk that you want to read in the drive and then mount the floppy disk drive.

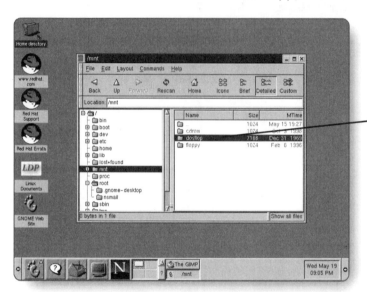

1. **Click** on the **Home Directory icon**. The File Manager will open and your home directory will be displayed.

2. **Open** either the **/mnt/dosflop or /mnt/floppy directory** depending of the type of formatted disk you want to read. You'll see the files on the floppy disk in the directory list.

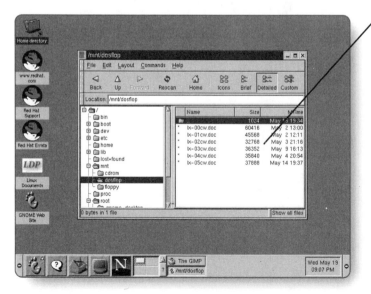

The files contained on the floppy disk will appear in the directory list. When you are finished with the floppy, close the file manager, unmount the floppy drive, and then you can take the disk out of the drive.

16

Adding Applications to Your Linux

Now that Linux is installed and configured on your computer, you can begin to enjoy some of its benefits. Linux is a wonderful playground with a wealth of things to do. Linux can help you with many of your tasks—you can use it both to install new applications and to upgrade old applications. You can also replace, update, or repair files in the installed programs. In this chapter, you'll learn how to:

- Verify that your applications are correctly installed
- Install the StarOffice application suite

Starting the GNOME RPM

The GNOME RPM or GnoRPM is a graphical front-end to the Red Hat Package Management System. Most Linux users will already be familiar with the Red Hat Package management system; but for those who aren't, the GnoRPM tool is the answer. You must be logged in as the superuser or root to install, upgrade, or uninstall applications. Users may verify and query packages to determine their status.

1. Place the **Red Hat Linux 6.0 Application CD** in your computer's CD-ROM drive. This is the special CD that comes with the boxed Red Hat Linux distribution and contains several software programs that you can try.

2. Mount the **CD-ROM drive**.

3. Click on the **Main Menu button**. The Main Menu will appear.

4. Move the **mouse pointer** to System. The System menu will appear.

5. Click on **GnoRPM**. The GNOME RPM window will open.

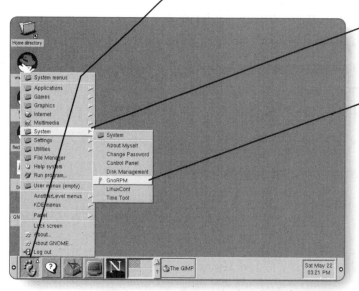

Take a minute to become familiar with the GNOME RPM window. The first packages that show up in the package panel are the packages that you already have on your system from the original installation.

- **Package panel.** This panel groups packages that perform similar functions into categories. These packages are applications that are available for you to install and use. Click on the plus sign next to a category to expand the list to show the subcategories.

- **Display window**. This window shows the different applications that are available in a selected category.

- **Status bar.** This bar shows how many packages are selected.

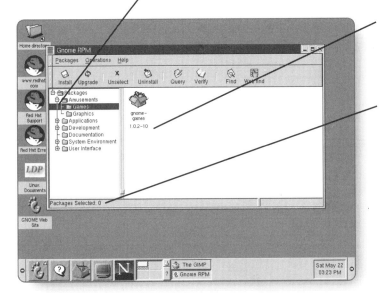

Verifying Installed Packages

If you suspect that one of your applications isn't working correctly, GNOME RPM is just the tool to verify it. GnoRPM is a graphical tool that verifies that an application is complete and working correctly. If needed, you can replace files and whole packages, as well as determine if all the packages available from the installation were installed.

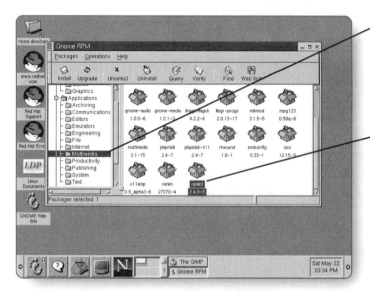

1. Click on the **category** in the Package Panel that contains the one that you want to verify. A list of the packages contained in that category will appear.

2. Click on a **package**. The package will be selected.

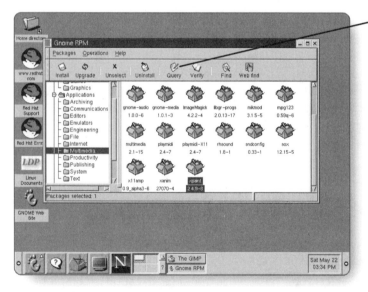

3. Click on the **Query button**. The Package Info dialog box will open.

In the Package Info dialog box, you can find out the build date of the package, its size, the files contained within it, and where they are installed in the Linux file system. At the bottom of the dialog box are buttons to verify the condition of the installed application package and to automatically install or uninstall packages after you have verified them.

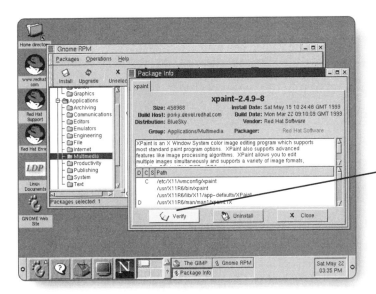

4. Click on the **Verify button**. The Verifying Packages dialog box will open.

The Verifying Packages dialog box will indicate the progress of the verification as the package is checked. If all the files in the package are intact, the dialog will return nothing. If one or more has become corrupted, it will be reported along with a description of the problem. You can then re-install the package and correct the problem.

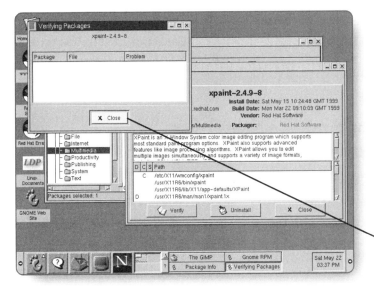

5. Click on the **Close button**. You'll return to the Package Info dialog box.

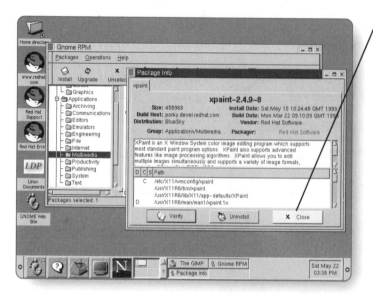

6. Click on the **Close button**. The package Info dialog box will close and you'll return to the GNOME RPM.

Installing a Package

The Package Management System provides the path and means for obtaining new applications and upgrades, as well as fixes for old applications and adding and removing modules to the Linux kernel. In this section, you're going to load an application from the Red Hat 6.0 Application CD and install it on your system.

Loading the StarOffice Application Suite

StarOffice is a suite of applications that provides tools for word processing, spreadsheet operations, and databases. Its output can be used with Microsoft Office applications. You'll install StarOffice from the Application CD that came with the boxed Red Hat 6.0 Linux.

1. Click on the **Upgrade button**. The Upgrade dialog box will open.

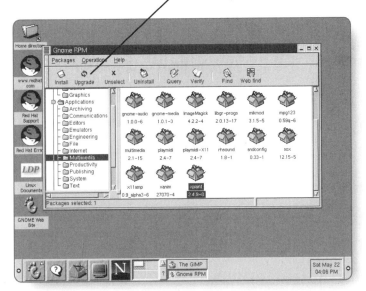

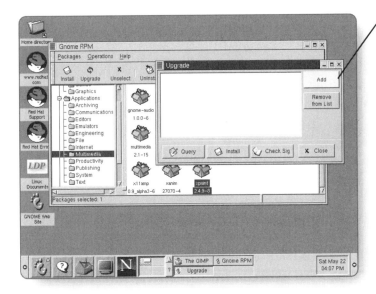

2. Click on the **Add button**. The Add Packages dialog box will open.

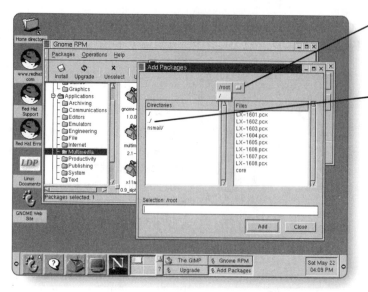

3. **Click** on the **directory drop down list button** next to /root. A list of directories will appear.

4. **Click** on **/**. This will take you to the root of your system.

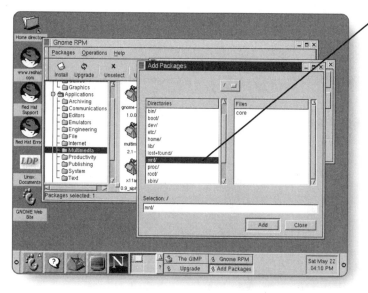

5. **Double-click** on **mnt/** in the Directories list. The contents of the mnt directory will appear.

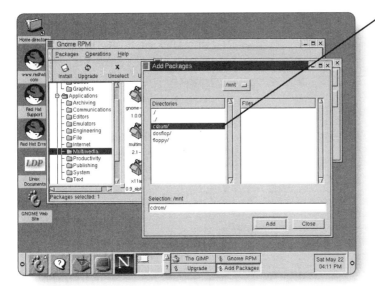

6. Double-click on the **cdrom/ directory**. The contents of the CD-ROM will appear.

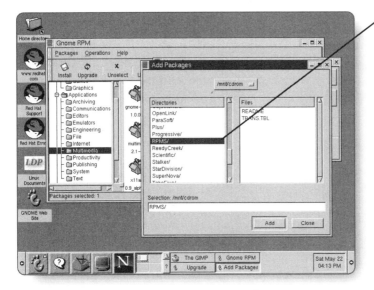

7. Scroll down the **Directories list** and **double-click** on the **RPMS/ directory**. The contents of the directory will appear.

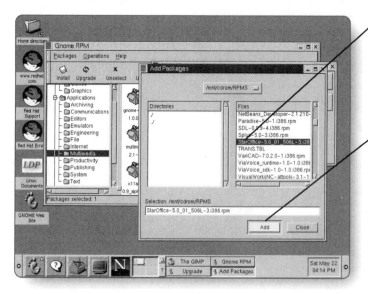

8. **Scroll down** the **Files list** and **click** on a **file**. To follow the figures, click on the StarOffice choice. The RPM for your selection will be selected.

9. **Click** on **Add**. Your selection will be added to the Upgrade list for packages that you want to install.

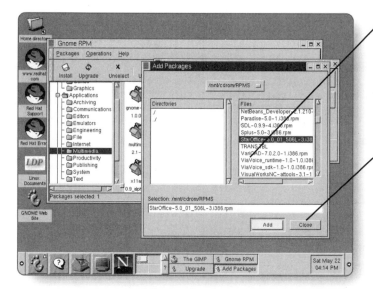

10. **Select** the **package** from the Files list if you want to install another package, and **click** on the **Add button**. The additional packages will be added to the Upgrade list.

11. **Click** on the **Close button**. The Add Packages dialog box will close and you will return to the Upgrade dialog box.

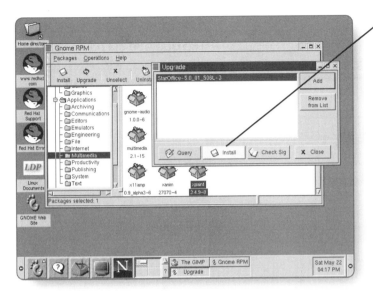

12. Click on the **Install button**. The Upgrading status box will open.

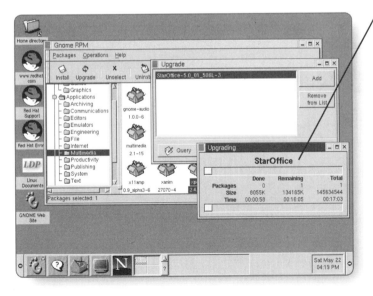

You'll see the program installing on your system. When the process is complete, the status box will close and you will return to the Upgrade dialog box.

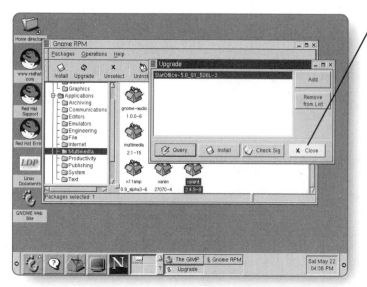

13. Click on the **Close button**. The Upgrade dialog box will close and you will return to the GNOME RPM.

14. Scroll down to the bottom of the **package panel** and click on the **plus sign** located to the left of X11. The list will expand.

15. Click on **Applications**. You'll see StarOffice in the display window.

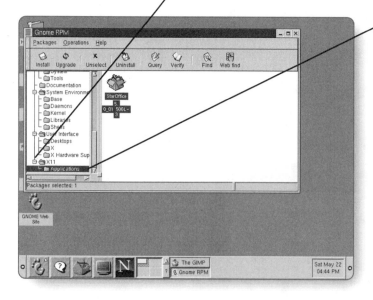

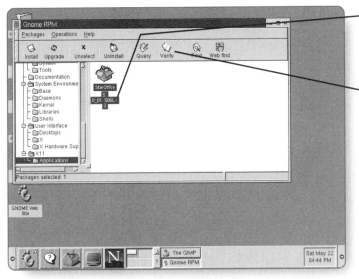

16. **Click** on the **StarOffice icon**. The StarOffice package will be selected.

17. **Click** on the **Verify button**. The Verifying Packages dialog box will open and will check to see if there were any problems with the installation. This may take a few minutes.

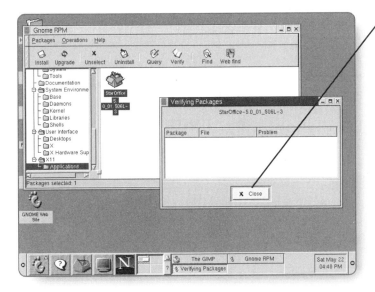

18. **Click** on the **Close button** when the verification is complete. The Verifying Packages dialog box will close and you'll return to the GNOME RPM.

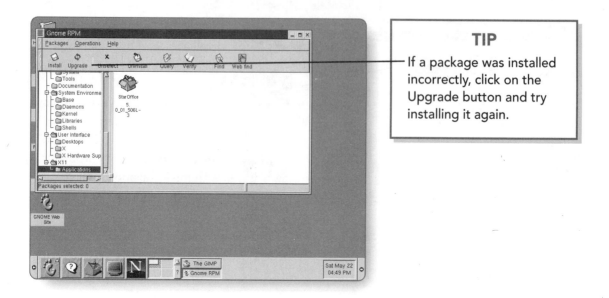

TIP

If a package was installed incorrectly, click on the Upgrade button and try installing it again.

19. Click on **Packages** when you are finished. The Packages menu will appear.

20. Click on **Quit**. The GNOME RPM will close. You will now need to register the program to finish the installation.

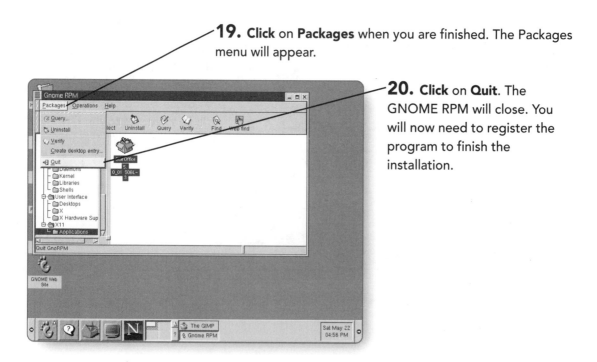

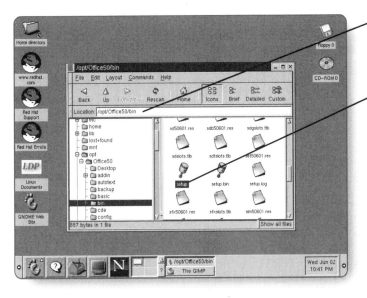

21. Open the **File Manager** and **navigate** to the **opt/Office50/bin/** directory.

22. Double-click on the **setup** file. A wizard will start and you'll need to follow the directions. When you are finished, each user will need to place a launch icon on their desktop.

Getting StarOffice to Your Desktop

Now that StarOffice is installed on your Linux system, it's time for users to put a StarOffice icon on their GNOME Panel so that they have access to the applications suite. To get started, log in as a user.

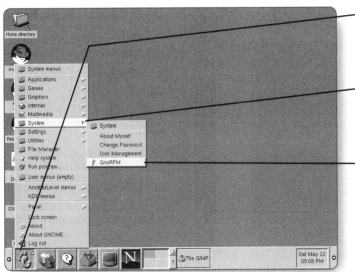

1. Click on the **Main Menu Button**. The Main Menu will appear.

2. Move the **mouse pointer** to System. The System menu will appear.

3. Click on **GnoRPM**. The GNOME RPM will open.

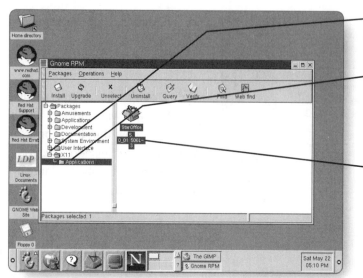

4. Click on the **plus sign** to the left of X11. The list will expand.

5. Click on **Applications**. The list of applications that can be added to the user's desktop will appear.

6. Click on the **StarOffice icon**. StarOffice will be selected.

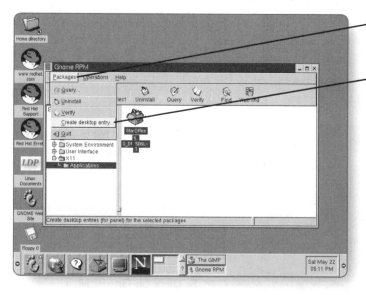

7. Click on **Packages**. The Packages menu will appear.

8. Click on **Create desktop entry**. The Desktop Entry Editor dialog box will open.

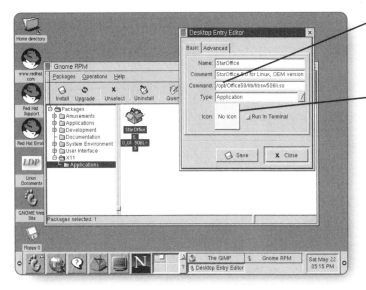

9. Change the **text** in the Command: text box to read /opt/Office50/bin/soffice.

10. Click on the **Icon button**. The Choose an icon dialog box will open.

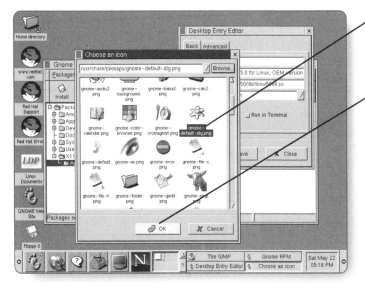

11. Click on the **icon** that you want to use for StarOffice. The icon will be selected.

12. Click on **OK**. You'll see the icon in the Icon box of the Desktop Entry Editor dialog box.

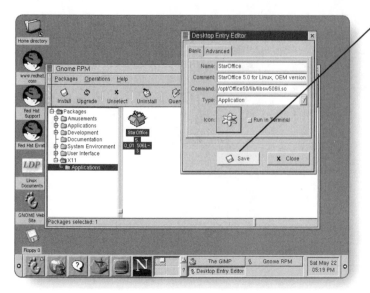

13. Click on **Save**. The Save Desktop Entry dialog box will open.

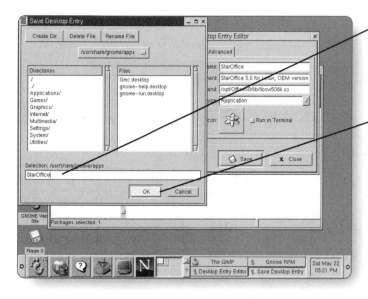

14. Type a **name** for the desktop entry (such as StarOffice) in the Selection text box.

15. Click on **OK**. You will return to the Desktop Entry Editor.

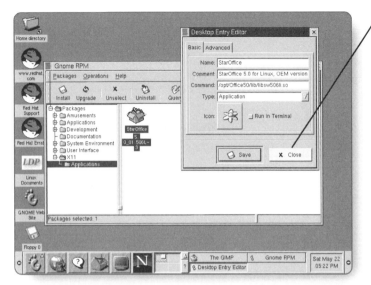

16. Click on the **Close button**. You will return to the GNOME RPM.

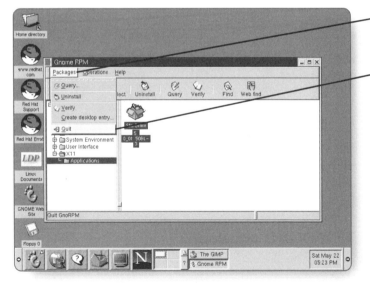

17. Click on **Packages**. The Packages menu will appear.

18. Click on **Quit**. The GNOME RPM window will close. To open StarOffice, you only need to click on the icon. The first time a user tries to open StarOffice, they will need to follow a wizard to install some files to their user account.

17

Getting On the Internet

Before you enter the Web, you'll need to set up an account with an Internet Service provider. The ISP will then provide some important information that is needed to set up the dial-up connection on your computer. You'll need a username or ID, password, access phone number, IP addresses, and mail and news server names. After you configure the connection, you can use the UserNet dialer utility to get connected. In this chapter, you'll learn how to:

- Set up your dial-up connection
- Connect to the Internet

Creating the Connection

Once an account is set up with an ISP and you have all the required information to create the dial-up connection, it is time to log into Linux as superuser or root and build a dial-up connection. This section will show how to configure the most popular connection, a PPP (*Point to Point Protocol*).

Setting Up a PPP Connection

You first must log in as root, and if you're using an external modem, make sure that the modem is turned on. Linux will automatically detect the location of your modem. You may want to check out the modem compatibility list at www.redhat.com/corp/support/hardware/intel/60/ rh6.0-hcl-i.ld-15.html before you begin. Certain modems do not work with Linux.

1. **Click** on the **Main Menu Button**. The Main Menu will appear.

2. **Move** the **mouse pointer** to the System menu. The System menu will appear.

3. **Click** on **LinuxConf**. The gnome-linuxconf window will open.

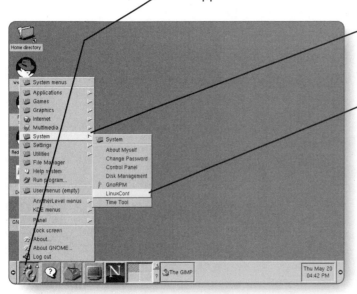

4. Look for the **Client tasks** category in the Networking section of the Config list.

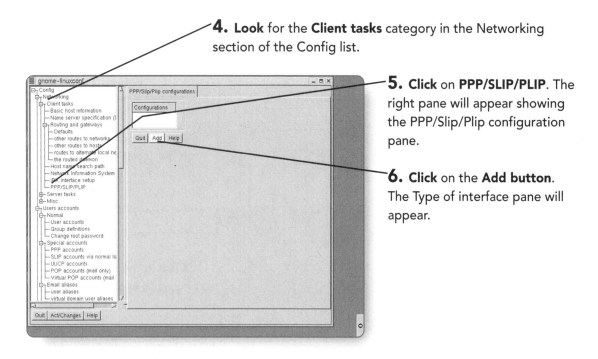

5. Click on **PPP/SLIP/PLIP**. The right pane will appear showing the PPP/Slip/Plip configuration pane.

6. Click on the **Add button**. The Type of interface pane will appear.

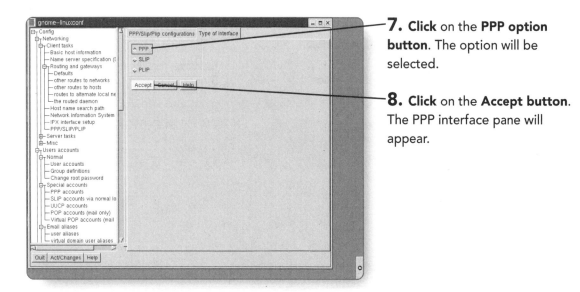

7. Click on the **PPP option button**. The option will be selected.

8. Click on the **Accept button**. The PPP interface pane will appear.

9. **Click** in the **Phone number text box** and **type** the **phone number** to access the Internet Service Provider. Do not use any spaces, parentheses or dashes—only numbers.

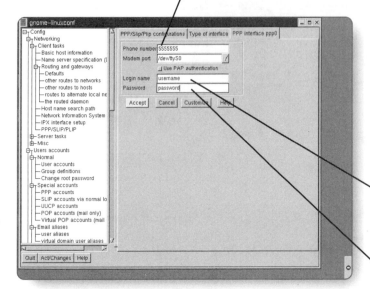

NOTE

If you need to dial a number (such as 9) to get an outside line or an area code, add that number before the phone number.

10. **Click** in the **Login name text box** and **type** the **login name** given to you by your ISP.

11. **Click** in the **Password text box** and **type** the **password** needed to access your ISP.

12. **Click** on the **Accept button**. You'll return to the PPP/Slip/Plip configurations pane and see your connection in the list of configurations.

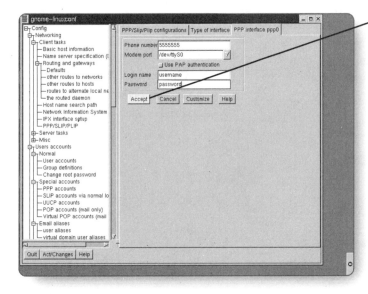

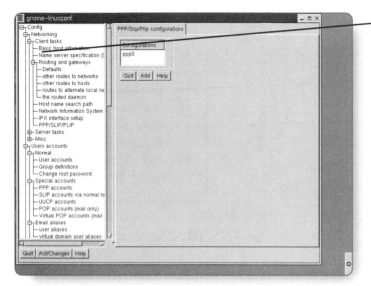

13. Click on the **Name server specification (DNS) option**. The Resolver configuration pane will appear.

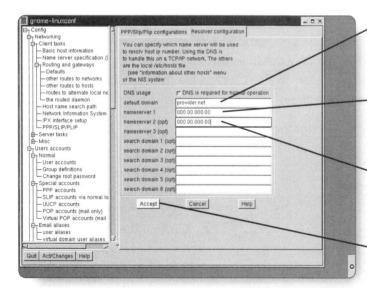

14. Click in the **default domain text box** and **type** the **domain name** of your ISP.

15. Click in the **nameserver 1 text box** and **type** the **DNS number** provided by your ISP.

16. Click in the **nameserver 2 (opt) text box** and **type** the **secondary DNS**.

17. Click on the **Accept button**. You'll return to the PPP/Slip/Plip configurations pane.

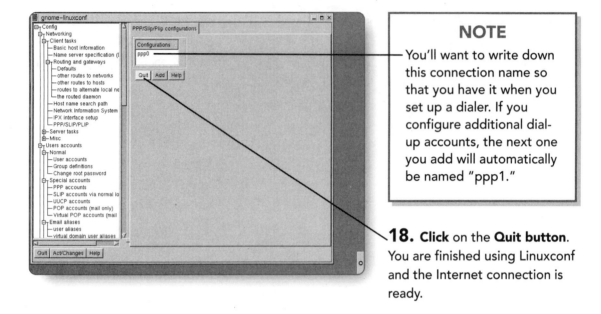

18. Click on the **Quit button**. You are finished using Linuxconf and the Internet connection is ready.

Giving Users Internet Access

You now have a dial-up connection configured for the entire system, but only the superuser has access to it. If you want to give the system users access to the dial-up connection, follow the next steps.

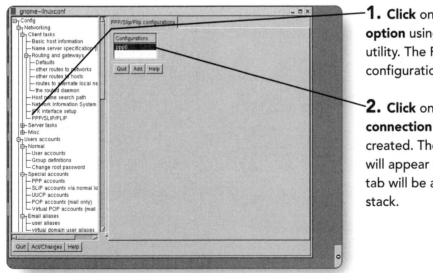

1. Click on the **PPP/SLIP/PLIP option** using the Linuxconf utility. The PPP/Slip/Plip configurations pane will appear.

2. Click on the **Internet connection** that you just created. The PPP interface pane will appear and the Hardware tab will be at the top of the stack.

TIP

You can check to see if your modem has been detected and will dial correctly by clicking on the Connect button.

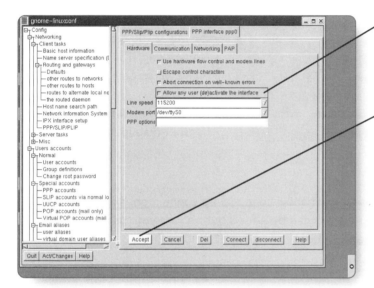

3. **Click** on the **check button** next to Allow any user to (de)activate the interface. The option will be selected.

4. **Click** on **Accept**. The Linuxconf utility will close and your users can now connect to the Internet through their own user account.

Connecting to Your ISP

After the dial-up connection has been configured, you can use the UserNet utility to dial up your ISP and make the Internet connection. The UserNet utility is a simple dialer that gets you connected in just a few short clicks. Remember, if you're using an external modem, make sure the modem is turned on.

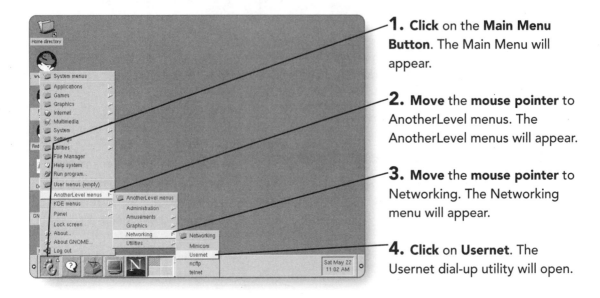

1. **Click** on the **Main Menu Button**. The Main Menu will appear.

2. **Move** the **mouse pointer** to AnotherLevel menus. The AnotherLevel menus will appear.

3. **Move** the **mouse pointer** to Networking. The Networking menu will appear.

4. **Click** on **Usernet**. The Usernet dial-up utility will open.

This Usernet shows one dial-up connection. Additional dial-up connections can be added but be sure your users know the difference between pp0, pp1, and pp2.

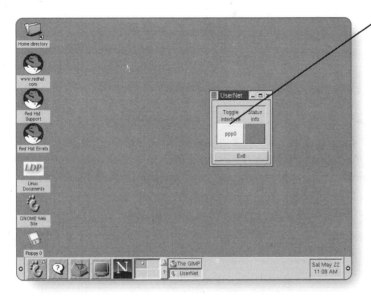

5. **Click** on the **Toggle interface button** for the dial-up connection that you want to access. The Status info button will change from red to yellow and the modem will dial. When the connection has been made, the Status info button will change to green and you'll be ready to go.

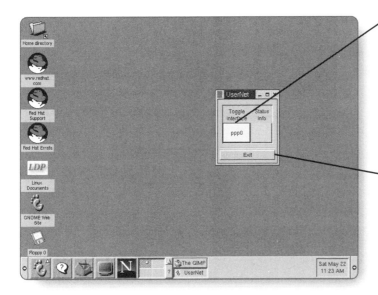

6. Click on the **Toggle interface button** for the active connection when you want to disconnect from the Internet. The Status info button will change from green to red and the modem will hang up.

7. Click on the **Exit button**. The UserNet utility window will close.

TIP

If you surf the Net often, you may want place the UserNet utility on the GNOME Panel as a launcher. See Chapter 5, "Managing Your Desktop," for a refresher.

18

Surfing the Web

Now that you've made the connection to your Internet Service Provider, you'll need a Web browser, e-mail program, and newsgroup reader so that you can travel on the Web and stay in contact with other people. You'll find all these capabilities, and more, in Netscape Communicator. If you've used the Windows or Macintosh version of Communicator, you'll feel right at home. For those who have worked with Microsoft Internet Explorer, this chapter can help you make the switch to Navigator. In this chapter, you'll learn how to:

- Use Netscape Navigator to visit Web sites
- Set up Communicator to access e-mail and newsgroups
- Send and receive e-mail
- Browse the newsgroups

Using the Netscape Navigator Web Browser

Netscape Navigator is one of several Linux Web browsers that you can use to surf the Web. If you come from a Windows or Macintosh background, you'll find Navigator to be a familiar face and a quick way to get up and running on the Web. Also, it's easy to find a launcher for Navigator.

1. Connect to your **Internet Service Provider**. You can use the UserNet utility from Chapter 17, "Getting on the Internet."

2. Click on the **Netscape Communicator icon** on the GNOME Panel. The Netscape Navigator Web browser will open.

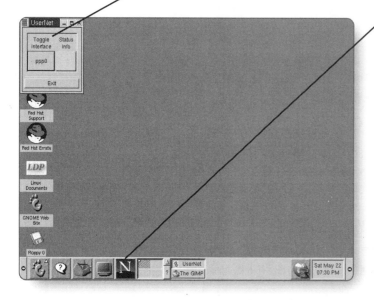

Accessing Web Pages

Begin by typing a Web address, or Uniform Resource Locator (URL), into the Location: text box. You may know of different addresses that you'd like to try, but if not, try the Prima Tech home page at www.prima-tech.com.

1. Double-click in the **Location box**. The URL (Uniform Resource Locator) that is currently in the Location box will be selected.

2. Type the **URL** of the Web page you want to visit. The first URL will disappear and the URL you type will display.

NOTE

It is not necessary to type the "http://" or "www" part of the address because Navigator will take care of that part.

---

3. Press the **Enter key** when you are finished typing the URL. The Web page will appear in the browser window.

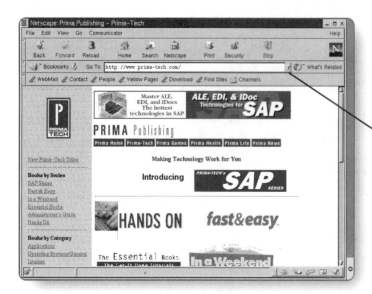

If you've typed Web addresses previously in the Location box, Navigator keeps track of these Web addresses in the Location box drop-down list.

4. Click on the **down arrow** to the right of the Location box. A list of URLs that you previously typed in the location box will appear.

5. Click on a **URL**. The associated Web page will appear in the browser window.

TIP

If you're searching for information and a page that you are visiting is close, but not quite what you were looking for, click on the What's Related button. A list of Web sites that are similar to the one currently displayed in the browser window will appear.

Changing Your Home Page

The home page is the first Web page you see when you open the Navigator browser. The first time you use Navigator, Red Hat creates a home page for you. You can change it to something that is more useful or interesting to you.

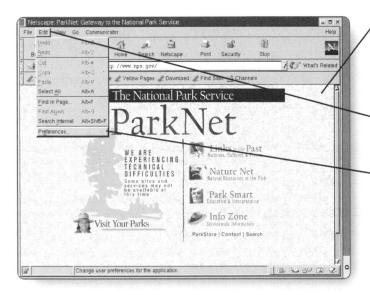

1. Open the **Web page** that you want to use as a home page. The Web page will appear in the browser window.

2. Click on **Edit**. The Edit menu will appear.

3. Click on **Preferences**. The Preferences dialog box will open.

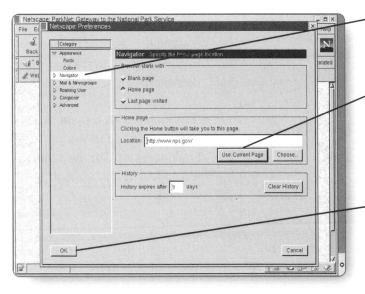

4. Click on the **Navigator category**. The Specify the home page location pane will appear.

5. Click on the **Use Current Page button**. The URL in the Location: text box will change to match the URL of the page displayed in the browser window.

6. Click on **OK**. The Preferences dialog box will close and you'll return to the browser window.

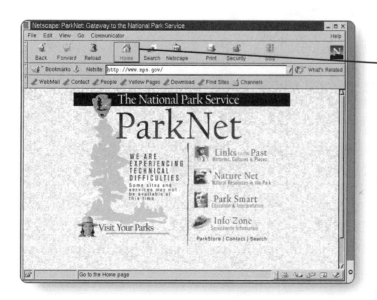

NOTE

When you're cruising around the Web, you can return to your home page easily with just a click of the Home button. Your default home page will appear in the browser window.

Keeping a List of Often Visited Web Sites

If you visit a number of Web sites on a regular basis, you'll want to keep of list of those sites for future references. A tool called Bookmarks will keep all the Web pages organized in one convenient place. If you don't want one big list of bookmarks, you can create folders in which to file the bookmarks.

1. Open the **Web page** that you want to add to the Bookmarks list. The Web page will appear in the browser window.

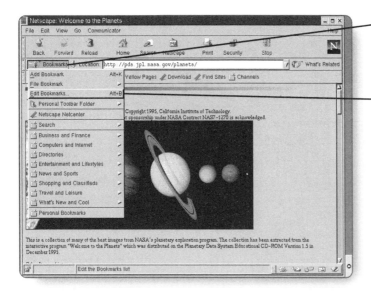

2. Click on the **Bookmarks button**. The Bookmarks menu will appear.

3. Click on **Edit Bookmarks**. The Communicator Bookmarks for [username] account dialog box will open.

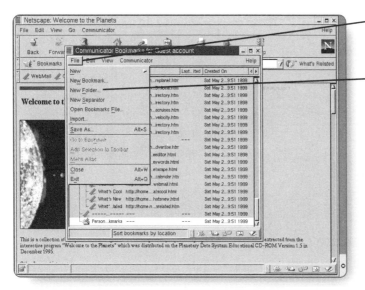

4. Click on **File**. The File menu will appear.

5. Click on **New Folder**. The Bookmark Properties dialog box will open.

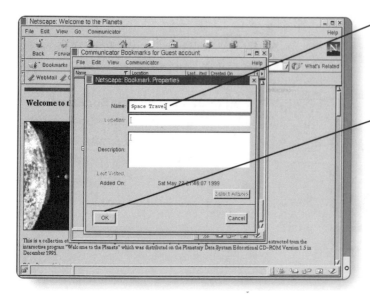

6. Select the **text** in the Name: text box and **type** a **name** for the folder in which you want to place some of your bookmarks.

7. Click on **OK**. The folder will be created.

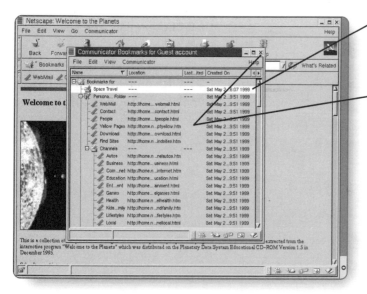

The new folder will appear in the bookmarks list and will be selected.

8. Click on the **Close button**. The Communicator Bookmarks dialog box will close and you're ready to file a bookmark into the folder.

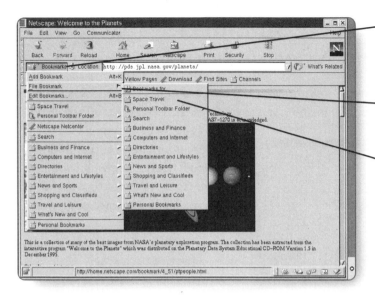

9. Click on the **Bookmarks button**. The Bookmarks menu will appear.

10. Click on **File Bookmark**. A second menu will appear.

11. Click on the **folder** into which you want to place the bookmark. The bookmark will be stored in the selected folder.

12. Click on the **Bookmarks button** to access a bookmark. The Bookmarks menu will appear.

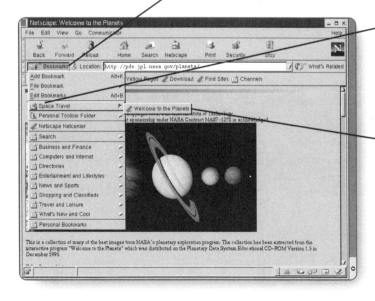

13. Click on the **folder** that contains the bookmark that you want to view. A list of the Web sites contained in the folder will appear.

14. Click on the **Web site**. The Web site will appear in the browser window.

Setting Up E-mail and News Accounts

When you set up your Internet account, the ISP assigned you a username and password to access their service. They should have also given you a mail server and news server address. You'll need these when you set up Communicator to work with e-mail and newsgroups.

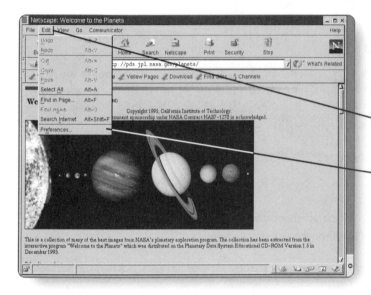

1. Click on **Edit**. The Edit menu will appear.

2. Click on **Preferences**. The Preferences dialog box will open.

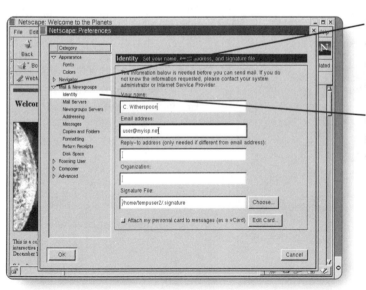

3. Click on the **arrow** next to the Mail & Newsgroups category. The category list will expand.

4. Click on the **Identity subcategory**. The Identity pane will appear.

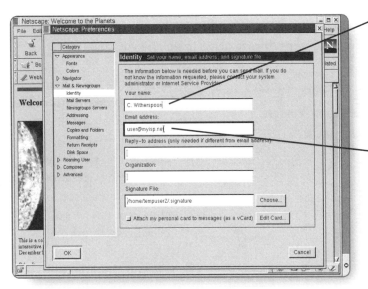

5. **Select** the **text** in the Your name: text box and **type** your **name**. What you type in this box is what will appear in the header information for all your outgoing messages.

6. **Select** the **text** in the Email address: text box and **type** your **e-mail address**.

7. **Click** on the **Mail Servers subcategory**. The Mail Servers pane will appear.

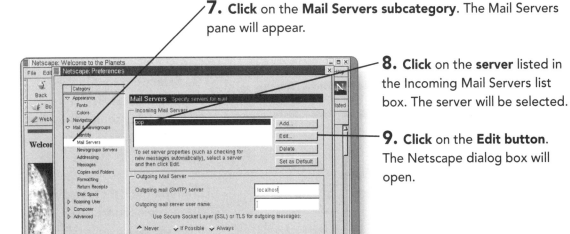

8. **Click** on the **server** listed in the Incoming Mail Servers list box. The server will be selected.

9. **Click** on the **Edit button**. The Netscape dialog box will open.

10. **Select** the **text** in the Server Name: text box and **type** the **mail server address** given to you by your ISP.

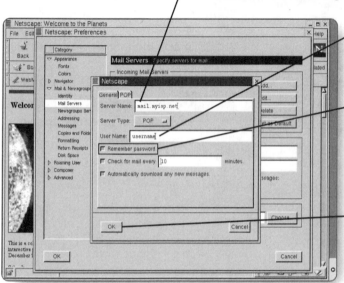

11. **Click** in the **User Name: text box** and **type** the **user ID** assigned to you by your ISP.

12. **Click** on the **check button** next to Remember password if you want Communicator to remember your password. The option will be selected.

13. **Click** on **OK**. You will return to the Preferences dialog box.

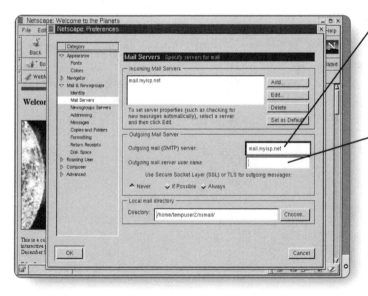

14. **Select** the **text** in the Outgoing mail (SMTP) server: text box and **type** the **outgoing mail server address** given to you by your ISP.

15. **Type** the **user name** in the Outgoing mail server user name: text box if your ISP requires a username for verification purposes when sending outgoing mail.

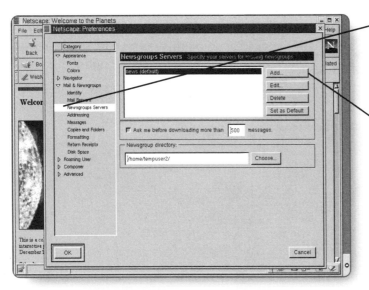

16. Click on the **Newsgroups Servers subcategory**. The Newsgroups Servers pane will appear.

17. Click on the **Add button**. The Netscape dialog box will open.

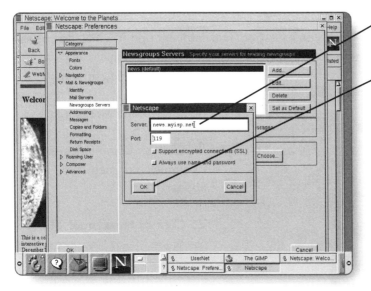

18. Type the **news server name** in the Server: text box.

19. Click on **OK**. The news server will be added to the list of servers.

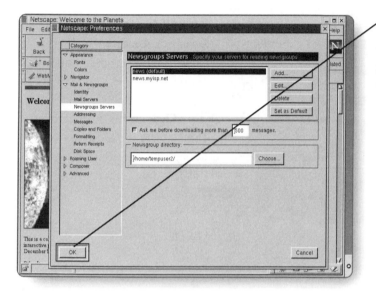

20. Click on **OK**. You're now ready to send and receive e-mail and browse through the newsgroups.

Managing E-mail

Now that you have Communicator set up for e-mail and news, it's time to go online and check to see if you have any messages waiting for you. Before you begin, you'll need to open Netscape Messenger.

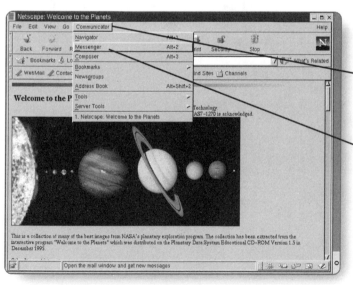

1. Click on **Communicator**. The Communicator menu will appear.

2. Click on **Messenger**. The Netscape Mail & Newsgroups window will open.

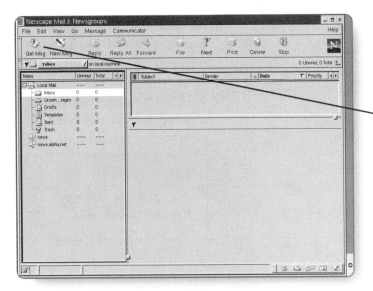

Receiving Messages

In just one click, all your e-mail will be delivered to you.

1. Click on the **Get Msg button**. A Password dialog box will appear.

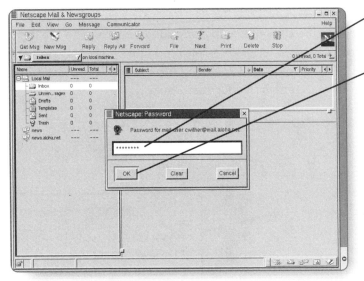

2. Type the **password** assigned to you by your ISP.

3. Click on **OK**. A download dialog box will appear and any new messages will be downloaded.

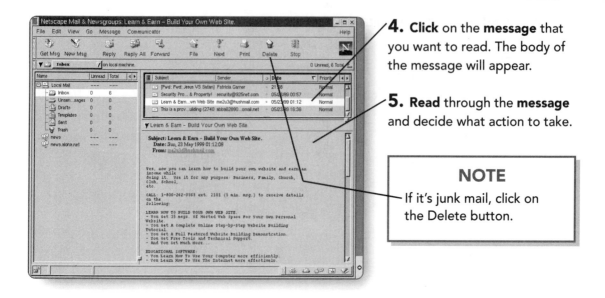

4. Click on the **message** that you want to read. The body of the message will appear.

5. Read through the **message** and decide what action to take.

> **NOTE**
> If it's junk mail, click on the Delete button.

Sending Messages

Gone are the days of stamps, envelopes, and trips to the post office. Now your letters are delivered to their recipient in a matter of seconds, and you don't have to make a special trip into town to replenish your stamp supply.

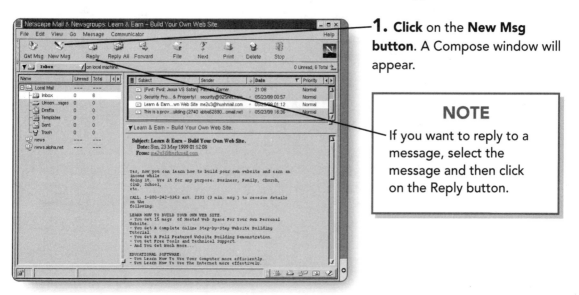

1. Click on the **New Msg button**. A Compose window will appear.

> **NOTE**
> If you want to reply to a message, select the message and then click on the Reply button.

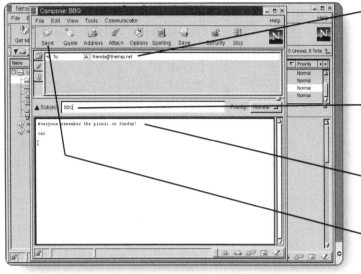

2. Type the **e-mail address** of the person to whom you want to send a message in the To: text box.

3. Type a **subject** for your message in the Subject: text area.

4. Type your **message** in the message pane.

5. Click on the **Send button**. Your message will be off to its intended recipient.

Lurking through the Newsgroups

Finding and joining one of the news bulletin board discussion groups on your favorite subject is easier than you think. With thousands of groups from which to choose, there's something in the newsgroups for everyone. If you want to learn more about computers, check out the myriad computer-related newsgroups. You can usually find someone willing to help you solve a problem, answer a question about how to use a software program, or discuss the future of computers.

Subscribing to Newsgroups

Before you can participate in newsgroup discussions, you'll need to make the newsgroup messages easy to view and readily available. You can do this by subscribing to the various newsgroups that interest you.

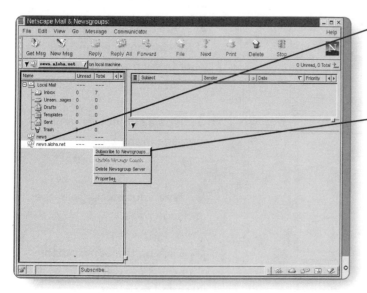

1. Right-click on the **news server** from which you want to download a list of newsgroups. A menu will appear.

2. Click on **Subscribe to Newsgroups**. The Netscape dialog box will open and the list of newsgroups will begin downloading from the server. This may take a while, depending on how many newsgroups are supplied by the news server. When the download has finished, the list of newsgroups will appear.

3. Click on the **Search tab**. The Search tab will come to the top of the stack.

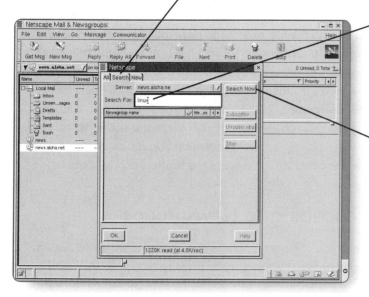

4. Type a **keyword** that describes the type of newsgroups in which you're interested into the Search For: text box.

5. Click on the **Search Now button**. Newsgroups that contain matching words will appear in the Newsgroup name list.

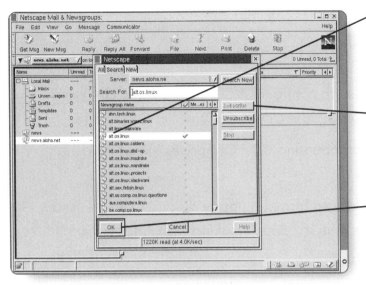

6. Click on the **newsgroup** to which you want to subscribe. The newsgroup will be highlighted.

7. Click on the **Subscribe button**. A check mark will appear to the right of the newsgroup name.

8. Click on **OK**. The newsgroup will appear under the news server in the Netscape Mail & Newsgroups window.

Reading Newsgroup Messages

To read the messages in the groups to which you have subscribed, follow these steps.

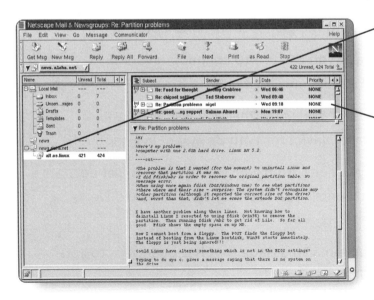

1. Click on the **name** of a subscribed newsgroup. The newsgroup headers will start downloading to your computer.

2. Click on the **newsgroup message** that you want to read. The message will open in the preview pane.

Part IV Review Questions

1. Which utility do you use to configure a CD-ROM so that Linux can access it? *See "Configuring the CD-ROM Drive" in Chapter 15*

2. What is the purpose of mounting CD-ROM drives? *See "Working with CDs" in Chapter 15*

3. Is it possible to use Linux to format a floppy disk that can be used on a DOS or Windows system? *See "Working with Floppy Disks" in Chapter 15*

4. How do you check to see if an application is installed correctly? *See "Verifying Installed Packages" in Chapter 16*

5. Where is one place that you can find applications to install on your Linux? *See "Installing a Package" in Chapter 16*

6. Which user on the Linux system has the ability to create an Internet connection? *See "Creating the Connection" in Chapter 17*

7. What is the easiest dialer you can use to connect to your ISP? *See "Connecting to Your ISP" in Chapter 17*

8. How can you keep a list of Web sites that you visit frequently? *See "Using the Netscape Navigator Web Browser" in Chapter 18*

9. What information do you need from your ISP in order to set up your mail and news accounts? *See "Setting Up E-mail and News Accounts" in Chapter 18*

10. How do you reply to an e-mail message that has been sent to you? *See "Managing E-mail" in Chapter 18*

P A R T V

Appendix

A

Installing Linux

Over the many Linux distributions since its beginning, much effort has been made to simplify the installation process. In the past, the long and involved installation process was a barrier that kept many people from installing and experimenting with Linux. Things are much better now and even somewhat automated, which takes a lot of the difficulty out of the task. However, even with an improved installation, you should still take the time to understand your computer's configuration and gain a little knowledge of what will happen during a Linux installation. Please read all the documentation before you begin. This appendix will show you how to perform the easiest Linux installation—running Linux as the sole operating system on your computer. In this appendix, you'll learn how to:

- Determine which installation method you want
- Prepare for the installation process
- Install the Red Hat Linux operating system

Understanding Your Installation Options

Linux is a very flexible operating system that can be easily modeled to meet your specific needs. Choices made during the installation process guide the setup program in selecting which software to load and configure. The installation process is enhanced by Linux's ability to probe your computer and provide answers to some of its own questions. Many of the choices you need to make are highlighted for you as you progress through the installation.

Another way in which the installation process has been simplified is the introduction of installation classes. You have three choices for the type of installation you can perform.

- The Workstation option is for those who are new to Linux and want an easy and automated installation. You'll also want to use this option if you are planning to use your Linux computer as a stand-alone workspace or as a workstation connected to a network.

- If you'll be using your Linux computer to run your network, you'll want to choose the Server option.

- If your requirements for the operation of your Linux computer do not really fit either of these two options, you may elect to install Linux by using the Custom option. You should be knowledgeable about your needs and have some experience configuring operating systems to use this option.

This appendix shows you a simple Workstation installation with Linux as the only operating system. If you have an old computer that doesn't seem to be performing well, this is a great opportunity to try out Linux, and add some useful life to an older computer. To write this book, we used a three-year old 133 Mhz Pentium II computer with 80 MB RAM. This computer has lived a hard life testing beta software for the past two years, and it was beginning to show signs of failure. The computer has been performing surprisingly well as a Linux machine.

Getting Ready

Before you begin, take time to plan and organize your Linux installation. If you come from a Windows or Mac background, you'll find a big learning curve ahead of you. But you'll also find that Linux has enormous potential. Please make sure that you understand the installation process and your computer's configuration before you begin. Read the Installation and Getting Ready manuals provided by Red Hat. Hit the Web and read through the Linux newsgroups, go to Red Hat's Web site and look at all of the resources available there.

You may want to think about keeping a Linux diary. Find a notebook or ring binder in which you can keep notes. Record everything you can about your computer's configuration. Write down the steps you followed during the Linux installation. Keep up with your Linux diary even after the installation. Keep notes about changes you made to the system, peripherals attached to the system, user accounts, problems you encountered, and any solutions.

Determining Your System Devices

To help Linux configure itself properly, and to help you avoid surprises, you need to collect some basic information about the hardware installed on your computer. This information may be found in the manuals that came with the computer or with the particular peripheral. It can also be obtained from the manufacturer or vendor. Or, If you have Microsoft Windows on your computer, you can look in the System Properties. And, remember, this is good stuff to keep in your Linux diary.

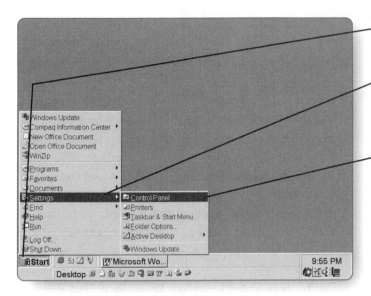

1. **Click** on **Start**. The Start menu will appear.

2. **Move** the **mouse pointer** to Settings. The Settings menu will appear.

3. **Click** on **Control Panel**. The Control Panel will appear.

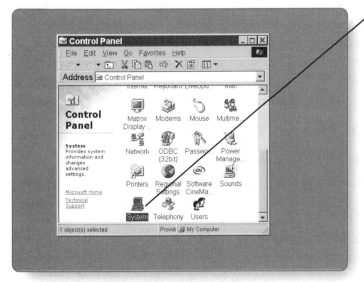

4. **Double-click** on the **System icon**. The System Properties dialog box will open.

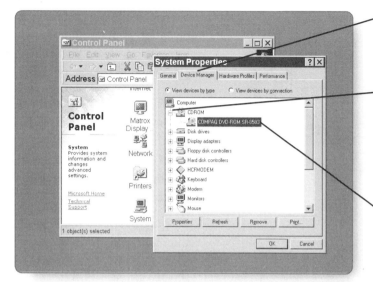

5. Click on the **Device Manager tab**. The Device Manager tab will come to the top of the stack.

6. Click the **Plus sign** next to a device. The device type will expand to show the devices of that type that are installed on your computer.

7. Click on the **device** about which you need hardware information. The device will be selected.

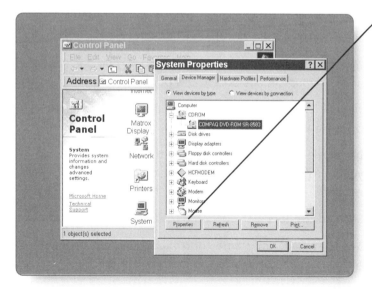

8. Click on the **Properties button**. The Properties dialog box for the selected device will open.

You'll need to know certain information about a number of devices. Write down the following information for each device:

- **CD-ROM drives**. Write down the interface type (IDE, SCSI, or other) and be sure and write down the manufacturer and model number of any in the 'other' category.

- **Display adapter**. You'll need the make and model and how much memory it has (most display adapters are autodetected).

- **Hard drives**. Write down the number of hard disk drives, how they are numbered, what size they are, and whether the drives are IDE or SCSI.

- **Modem**. Take down the make and model number, speed, and communications port (COM port).

- **Mouse**. What kind of mouse is yours? A PS-2 compatible one or a serial mouse, with one, two, or three buttons?

- **Network adapters**. You will need the information about your card's make and model if you are to be connected to a network.

- **SCSI controllers**. Jot down the make and model numbers.

- **Sound, video, and game controllers**. Find out the names of the manufacturers and the model numbers.

- **Monitor**. You should know your monitor's make and model number and the vertical and horizontal refresh rate parameters.

Now that you have all this information, you need to check your computer hardware with the Red Hat Linux Hardware Compatibility List. You can find it on the Web at www.redhat.com/corp/support/hardware/index.html. If you have incompatible hardware, try to determine how this will affect the installation before you begin. You'll find very few modems that are compatible. Linux couldn't find our internal modem, so we purchased an external modem. Another common installation problem is sound cards.

There are other Web resources that you should look into before you begin. Try out the various newsgroups. Red Hat has a number of user groups that you can join. You can find these groups at www.redhat.com/usergroups. There's also some useful information on the Red Hat Linux 6.0 CD number 1. Look in the DOC directory.

Formatting the Linux Drive

If you'll be using Linux as the sole operating system, you'll need to run the MS-DOS fdisk utility on the drive to prepare it for the installation. If the drive has been formatted or partitioned before, you'll need to remove the old partitions. To remove DOS partitions, it is best to use the MS-DOS fdisk utility, as it seems to work better than the Linux fdisk on DOS drives.

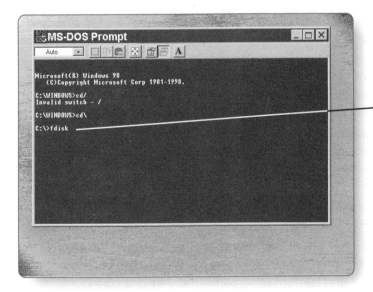

1. **Format** a **floppy disk**.

2. **Copy** the **system files** to the disk.

3. **Find** the **fdisk.exe file** (probably located in the Windows/Commands directory)

4. **Copy** the **fdisk.exe file** to the floppy disk.

5. **Restart** your **computer** with the floppy disk in the disk drive. When your computer restarts, you'll have a DOS prompt.

6. **Type fdisk** and **press Enter**. A message about large disk drives may appear.

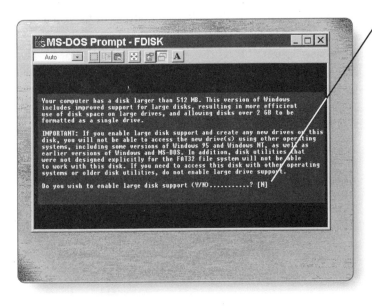

7. **Type N** so that large disk drive support is not enabled and **press Enter**. The FDISK Options screen will appear.

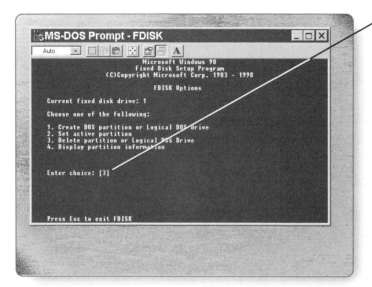

8. Type 3 and **press Enter**. The Delete DOS Partition or Logical DOS Drive screen will appear.

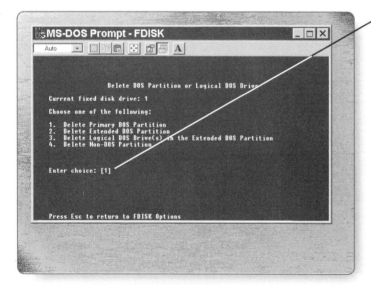

9. Type 1 and **press Enter**. This will delete all the information on your hard drive. The Delete Primary DOS Partition screen will appear.

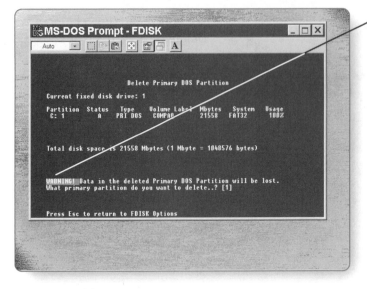

10. **Type** the **number** of the primary DOS partition that you want to delete and **press Enter**. The information at the top of the screen will help you make this decision. The Enter Volume Label text box will appear.

11. **Type** the **Volume Label** as it appears in the description at the top of the screen and **press Enter**. A confirmation line will appear.

12. **Type Y** and **press Enter**. The contents of the drive will be deleted.

13. **Press** the **Escape key**. The FDISK Options screen will appear.

14. **Press** the **Escape key** until you return to a DOS prompt.

Loading the Linux Operating System

Now's the moment you've been waiting for. You've read all the documentation, learned everything you can about your computer and peripherals, and prepared a hard drive just for the Linux installation. It's time to grab that CD and get the show on the road.

Insert the Red Hat Linux 6.0 CD-ROM number 1 into your computer's CD-ROM drive and insert the Linux Boot Disk into your floppy drive. Turn off the power to your computer, wait 15 seconds, and then turn on the power. Your computer will restart.

When your computer reboots, a Welcome screen will appear. Press the Enter key and you'll see a series of text lines appear across your screen. You'll want to wait while these software drivers load. When this is finished, another welcome screen will appear. Press the Enter key.

You'll then see a series of three dialog boxes that need some basic information before the installation process can begin. You'll need to choose your language, keyboard, and location of the Linux installation files. Press the Up and Down Arrow keys on the keyboard to select an option. When your option is highlighted, press the Enter key. You'll move to the next screen. If you are installing from a CD-ROM drive, you may be asked to insert the CD-ROM into the drive. The installation will begin.

The Installation Path screen will appear. This screen asks whether you are upgrading an earlier installation of Linux on your machine or if you are making an original full installation of the operating system. If this is the first time you've installed Linux, select the Install option. Press Tab to move the cursor so that your choice is highlighted, and press Enter to select the highlighted option. Your choice will be saved and you will be moved to the Installation Class screen.

Here you will make the choice of the type of installation you want. Select Workstation from the list and press Enter. Two warning screens will appear. For the first warning screen, select OK and press Enter. For the second warning screen, select the Yes option and press Enter. The installation will begin.

Because you selected the Workstation class installation, the installation will begin with Linux making its own partitions on your hard drive and installing the packages, tools, and utilities you will need. You'll see a series of installations going on in the Install Status dialog box. Watch this and you'll see all the nifty programs that are being installed along with your Linux. This may take about 15–20 minutes, depending on the speed of your computer.

When the installation is complete, a Probing Result screen will appear. This will happen when the Linux system finds a device such as a mouse or monitor. Press Enter to display the configure screen for the device. Scroll through the list and select the option that most closely matches the type of device. Then press Enter. The Network Configuration screen will appear.

If you are setting up this machine as a stand-alone workstation and will be connecting to the Internet with a dial-up connection, select the No option on the Network Configuration screen and press Enter. The Configure Timezones screen will appear.

Now you'll need to set the time zone in which you live. Select your time zone from the list, select the OK option, and press Enter. The Configure Printer screen will appear.

You may or may not want to set up a printer at this time (see Chapter 13, "Printing Files"). For now, select No and press Enter. The Root Password screen will appear.

You'll need to set a root password. It is important that you pick one that you will remember and one that won't be easily compromised because the root password allows the user entry to the entire system. Type a password twice; press the Tab key between fields. Select the OK option and press Enter. You'll need to remember this password so that you can log into Linux. The Bootdisk screen will appear.

You'll be asked if you want to create a boot diskette. You may use it in emergencies to boot your system. Select the Yes option and press Enter. The Bootdisk screen will appear. Place a blank floppy disk in your floppy disk drive and press Enter. An emergency boot disk will be created for your Linux system. When the boot disk is created, you may get a series of PCI Probe screens.

The system that controls the operation of your computer monitor and video card when you are running Linux is the Xwindow system. The version of Xwindows installed with Linux operating system is called Xfree86. The Xfree86 configuration file needs to be modified to let Linux know which X server to load to make the best use of your hard The installation screens walk you through the configuration and may ask you to provide information about your monitor and video card.

CAUTION

When configuring Xwindows for your computer, it is possible to permanently damage your monitor and/or video card by entering the wrong information! If you are not truly knowledgeable about configuring video and operating systems, now is not the time to try to guess the answer.

Now before you panic, the Red Hat installation program has the ability to probe your system and autodetect all or most of the information needed. You then only have to select a few things from lists and the whole thing will flow smoothly.

Red Hat's installation program will probe your hardware to determine what video equipment you have installed. In most cases, the probe will return all the information it needs about your video card and monitor. That is what we always want to happen, but there are exceptions and sometimes you need to get a little more involved in the configuration process. If you need to help Linux configure Xfree86, you will be presented with a series of screens to guide you.

You'll be asked to select your monitor from a list. If you can't find yours listed, you'll be asked to select a generic monitor from a list of monitor descriptions. If this is the case, the

Information that you collected about your monitor's horizontal and vertical sync rates will come in handy when you select them from the two following dialog screens.

Make conservative choices and leave yourself a margin of safety. In other words, if the numbers you have collected for your monitor show the vertical scan rate range to be 50hz to 90hz, the range you select needs to match that or be inside that range.

Once you have selected your monitor or finished that portion of the Xwindow installation, you will be asked if you would like for the computer to test your choice.

The Red Hat installation widget will probably have already gathered all of the information that it needs about your video card. But, if not, you'll be asked to select your card from a list and perhaps add some information that the installation program didn't autodetect.

Once again, you will be asked if you want the installation program to run a probe to see if your video is configured right. Select yes, and the information from the probe will be used to select the proper X server for your card and monitor.

At the end of the configuration wizard, the program returns information about which X server is loaded and what screen resolutions are available for you to use. You may select several resolutions and color depths that you can switch back and forth.

TIP

If you entered the wrong monitor or video card information, you may not be able to start Xwindows. To return to Xconfigurator to fix your mistake, press Ctrl+Alt+Backspace.

Glossary

A

absolute path. Specifies the exact directory in the directory tree where a file or subdirectory is stored. The absolute path includes the entire path that is required to access the file. The absolute path begins with the root directory.

access rights. These are also known as file permissions. These define which users have access to which files, directories, and peripherals in the system, and the type of access each user is allowed.

active window. The window in which an application will run or in which a task will be performed.

anonymous FTP. A way in which any person can access the public areas of an FTP site to transfer data files. To access these public areas, use "anonymous" as the user name and your e-mail address as the password.

application. A software program that performs a specific task or function, such as word processing, bookkeeping, or graphics.

archive. To put data files in a place where they are protected from loss. Use a backup program to copy the files onto a removable media that can be kept in a safe deposit box or fireproof safe.

B

background process. A function (such as a print job or automatic save) that does not require interaction from the user. When a function is running in the background, the user can work with another application without any noticeable effect on performance.

backup. To make a copy of files that are stored on the computer's hard drive onto another medium, such as a floppy disk, magnetic tape, or CD-ROM. If the files on the hard disk become damaged or lost, it is possible to restore the files from the backup.

boot. The process your computer goes through when it is turned on so that the operating system loads.

boot disk. A floppy disk that is created during the installation process so that the Linux operating system can start in the event that the Linux Loader (LILO) does not work on the system.

boot image floppy. A floppy disk that will boot the computer and load a small Linux operating system. This floppy disk may be needed before installation of the entire Linux distribution.

C

cache memory. A storage area for data as it moves between the computer's RAM memory and the processor chip. Cache memory is needed to keep the processor working at full potential. Most computers have either 128K or 256K of cache memory. This speed indicates how fast the processor moves data in and out of cache memory.

command line. This is a text mode display where Linux commands are typed and then executed by pressing the Enter key. Command line operations can be performed from a terminal window, a terminal emulator, a console, or an x-term window. The easiest to work with is the x-term window because it can be opened inside the GNOME interface and it is not necessary to log out of the interface to perform functions that cannot be executed with the interface.

current directory. The directory or folder in which all file and directory commands operate. The current directory will usually be the Home directory.

D

daemon. A process that sits in the background and waits until something activates it. For example, the update daemon starts on a regular cycle to flush the buffer cache; the Sendmail daemon starts when mail is sent over the network.

defragment. A computer maintenance task that reorganizes the file system so that programs run efficiently and files are located and displayed quickly. The program locates files that are scattered throughout a hard drive, combines the pieces into one file, and prioritizes them on the hard drive according to usage.

desktop. The background that displays behind all the different screen elements (such as windows, dialog boxes, and applications) used in the Linux operating system.

device drivers. Small software programs that provide access to system devices and resources such as disk drives, modems, graphics cards, and printers.

dial-up networking. A method of connecting to the Internet or to some other computer or network through a dial-up modem.

directory. A unique address in the computer's file system where files are stored. Linux uses several conventions for indicating the location of the directory in relation to other directories. Directories and subdirectories are separated by a forward slash (/), which is different from DOS and Windows systems. A single forward slash indicates that the user is at the root directory. The current directory in which the user is working is indicated by a single period (.). The directory that is above the current directory is indicated by two periods (..).

distribution. A set of prepackaged Linux software made available by a vendor. The package contains the Linux operating system, the set of GNU software applications and utilities, and other software programs developed by the vendor.

dynamic IP address. An Internet Protocol address assigned when the dial-up connection is made. This means that each time the user connects to the Internet, the user will get a different IP address.

E

encryption. A procedure used in cryptography to convert text into cipher to keep anyone but the intended recipient from reading the message. There are many types of data encryption that are the basis of network security. Data Encryption Standard and public key encryption are common.

executable file. A single file used to open a program.

F

FDISK (DOS). A DOS utility that allows the creation and management of partitions on a hard disk drive. There are many places to access the FDISK utility, but the most common is to use the FDISK utility that is installed with the operating system controlling the hard drive that is to be partitioned. This is the one to use to partition a DOS drive so that both Windows and Linux can share the same drive.

FDISK (Linux). A Linux disk managing utility, like the fdisk (DOS) utility, that is used to manage Linux drives. This is the utility to use after the partition of the drive into a DOS partition for Windows and a non-DOS partition for Linux. The Linux FDISK utility will be used to partition the non-DOS part of the drive for the Linux file system.

file. A collection of data, such as a letter created in a word processing program or a scanned image of a photograph, that is stored on a hard drive or other storage medium.

file permissions. A way to protect files from being tampered with by other users on a computer or network. The user who creates the files owns the files and the directories in which the files are contained. The owner can specify which other users may have access to the files and the type of access.

file server. A computer that maintains data files and allows users and other computers in the network to access those files to which they have permission.

file system. The method and data structure that the Linux operating system uses to store files. The file system can be used to organize and manage files.

foreground process. The application in which the user is currently working. A foreground process receives input from the keyboard and the results are seen on the screen.

Free Software Foundation. A grant-sponsored group at MIT that develops and distributes software for UNIX operating systems. The Free Software Foundation has developed such products as X Windows, emacs, a C++ compiler, and the glib++ library. They are well known for all of their GNU software.

FTP (File Transfer Protocol). A method of sending and receiving files across a computer network or the Internet.

G

GNOME (GNU Network Object Model Environment). A graphical user interface that makes it easier to work with the Linux operating system. GNOME makes it easy to run programs, access frequently used files, and find utilities that are included in the operating system.

GNOME Panel. The bar at the bottom of the screen (using the GNOME interface) that contains the Main Menu button, customizable panel applets, and the GNOME Pager. These elements are a quick way to access frequently used programs and files.

GNU project. A project sponsored by the Free Software Foundation to provide a freely distributable replacement for UNIX. Some of the more popular tools are the GNU C and C++ compilers and the GNU EMACS editor.

GUI (Graphical User Interface). A shell that runs over the Linux operating system. This shell allows a user to visually see the operating system in action rather than by using commands. The shell uses windows, dialog boxes, icons, and other graphics to create an environment which is easier to work in. A GUI also supports the use of the mouse to make tasks easier.

H

home directory. The place within the Linux file system where the user stores or saves all the files and directories (or folders) that the user creates.

I

icon. A small picture that represents an application, peripheral, file, or directories.

K

kernel. The center of the Linux operating system. This piece of software is responsible for the Linux file system and the timing activities of the operating system. Operating system utilities use kernel functions to perform work. The kernel is recompiled occasionally when system changes require it.

kernel patch. To create a new binary file for the core Linux operating system.

L

LILO (Linux Loader). A program that resides in the boot sector of the hard disk. LILO executes when the computer system is turned on and automatically boots up the Linux operating system from a kernel image stored on the hard drive.

linking loader. A single program that loads, relocates, and links compiled and assembled programs, routines, and subroutines to create an executable file. Also known as link loader and linker loader.

log on/log off. To connect to or disconnect from a network such as the Internet or a corporate intranet. Also, to access a specified user account in the Linux system. Logging on requires a user name and a password.

M

Main Menu button. The button located on the GNOME Panel that looks like a foot. This button displays a menu containing applications, utilities, the File Manager, help, and log out options.

Man pages. Information pages contained in Linux that contain documentation for the system commands, resources, configuration files, and other utilities.

Master Boot Record. The file used to boot the computer's operating system and configure it for all the peripherals and utilities.

minimize. To clear a window from the desktop and cause it to become an icon on the GNOME Pager. To display the window, click on its icon on the GNOME Pager.

mount. A task that is performed before a device; for example, a floppy disk drive or CD-ROM drive can be accessed by the Linux file system.

O

operating system. Software that shares a computer system's resources such as the processor, memory, and disk space between users and the application programs that run.

P

panel applet. An icon on the GNOME Panel that launches a program or opens a file.

partition. A physical portion of a disk. Disks are divided into partitions that are assigned to hold various file systems. The root file system is usually on the first partition and the user file system is on a different partition. The use of partitions provides flexibility and control of disk usage, but is restricting in that it denies unlimited use of all available space on a given disk for a given file.

password. A personal secret code word or series of numbers used to log onto the Internet, access a network account, or work with files that are protected from general view.

path. A file name given as a sequence of directories that leads to a particular file.

R

root directory. The base directory from which all other subdirectories stem.

S

static IP address. An unchanging IP address, usually for those that are permanently connected to the Internet.

superuser. The root or administrator account who has the ability to access the entire Linux system and any user accounts that have been set up. The superuser account is used by the Linux system manager to install software, fix problems, and perform backup routines.

swap space. A place on the computer hard disk drive that is set aside so that it can be used as virtual memory (extra RAM). Linux uses this swap space to store programs that may be running. This swap space is dedicated to virtual memory and cannot be accessed to store files for directories.

U

unmount. To remove a file system that has been previously mounted. Only the user or superuser who mounted the file system can unmount it.

user. A person who uses the Linux system and has been assigned a user account.

V

virtual memory. To use part of the hard disk to extend the amount of RAM the computer can use. When the computer has used the available RAM, it takes the contents of memory that are not needed to process current tasks and places that information on the hard drive.

W

window. A rectangular area displayed when an application runs on the screen. There can be many windows displayed on the screen at any time. Windows can be moved, resized, closed, minimized, and opened with the click of the mouse.

window manager. The software that controls the way windows look, their functionality, and where they are placed in the GNOME interface. The GNOME interface that is installed with Red Hat Linux 6.0 works with the Enlightenment Window Manager.

X

Xwindows. The graphical system that is used by every Linux and UNIX operating system. This graphical system provides an interface to video hardware, manages windows and other objects on the screen, and controls the desktop (such as GNOME or KDE).

Index

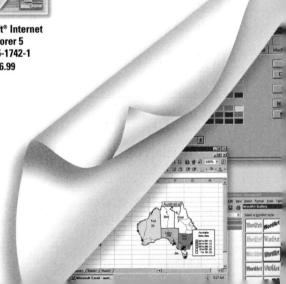